LIFE AFTER DEBT

Christianity and Global Justice

Michael Northcott

First published in Great Britain in 1999 by
SPCK, Holy Trinity Church, Marylebone Road,
London NW1 4DU

© Michael Northcott 1999

Scripture quotations are from the *New Revised Standard
Version of the Bible* © 1989.

British Library Cataloguing-in-Publication Data
A catalogue record for this book is available from the British Library

ISBN 0-281-05077-5

Photoset by Wilmaset, Birkenhead, Wirral
Printed in Great Britain by
Biddles Ltd, Guildford and King's Lynn

Contents

Acknowledgements

I am very grateful to those who encouraged me to write this book, and in particular to Michael Taylor and Paul Spray, formerly of Christian Aid, and Duncan Forrester and Andrew Morton at the Centre for Theology and Public Issues in Edinburgh. I am also grateful to those who read and commented on drafts of the manuscript and in particular Mark Birchall, Rebecca Dudley, Duncan Forrester, Jeoman George, Roger Jeffrey, M. P. Joseph, Jolyon Mitchell, Jenny Robertson, Nicolas Sagovsky, Gillian Weeks and Roger Williamson. I have tried to take on board their very helpful criticism and advice but of course any inaccuracies which remain are my own. Finally I want to thank all those staff and students who have been involved in the M.Th. course in Theology and Development here in the Faculty of Divinity in the University of Edinburgh since 1990. It has been a privilege to teach on this course and to get to know the many church development workers from Africa, Asia and Central America who have come to Scotland to reflect on their experiences. This book emerged from seminars in which we together struggled with the theological and ethical implications of debt, trade, sustainability and globalization, and the complex legacy of colonialism and post-colonialism with which they are intertwined.

The style of the book was suggested to me on reading Theodore Zeldin's *An Intimate History of Humanity* (London: Minerva, 1995) in which, through the stories of women in France, Zeldin illuminates the roots and character of many of the cultural, emotional and personal features of modern life and experience. In the present book each chapter also commences with a story which is designed to draw the reader into direct engagement with the subject of the chapter through personal encounter. The stories mostly draw on the verbatim testimony of real people involved in real events but the names of the individuals have been changed to protect their identities. It is important also to note that the stories are composites drawing on the testimony of more than one individual interviewed by Christian Aid staff. In establishing the location and setting I have mostly drawn on the words of the Christian Aid staff who visited the places where the cases are set, some of whom helpfully embellished their written accounts in telephone conversations with me. The stories are also mostly the stories of women. This is intentional because it is often women who suffer most from the discrimination and oppressive conditions which characterize the life of the poor under the exigencies of debt, structural adjustment and the global deregulation of international trade. The first and last chapters are different, however. Jeremy and Joseph's stories are inventions, though based on published accounts and oral testimony from individuals who know the settings.

Each chapter investigates the issues raised by the story, first through an engagement with the literature on the economics and politics of development and globalization, and secondly through a consideration of theological resources drawn from the Christian tradition, and particularly from the growing tradition of contextual theologies from the South. Each chapter concludes with information about organizations which readers may want to contact concerning the issues raised.

Michael S. Northcott
New College
University of Edinburgh

Foreword

Michael Northcott's book is most timely. Its publication just as the second millennium is drawing to a close, and as the year of the Jubilee approaches, is intended to remind us all of the relevance but also the significance of the law of Jubilee.

The term Jubilee, at least in the English language, is seen as an injunction to celebrate. And for many the new millennium will be a time for celebration. Those who live in the North, for example, could celebrate this stark fact: that between 1985 and 1995 the five richest countries of the world increased their GNP per capita by 100 per cent. For those in the poorest countries, however, there is less to celebrate. The ten most impoverished countries were stripped of 30 per cent of their annual per capita income over this period.

Debt bondage has been the key mechanism for enriching the five richest countries, and for impoverishing the ten poorest. Countries in hock to Western creditors have no choice but to do their bidding: namely, to open up their markets to Western goods; to restrict the production of value-added goods that compete with Western exports; to accept appropriation by foreign conglomerates of their most valuable state assets; and to skew their economies in ways which satisfy the demands of their creditors. We no longer have debtors' prisons for people; we have them for countries instead. Countries as different as Zambia and Brazil – who have over-borrowed on the international capital markets (or had loans pushed at them) and find income for repayment falling precipitously (because dollars earned through commodity exports have collapsed) – have no choice. They have to subordinate their economies to international bankers and governmental creditors. These are all represented by a relatively small but key creditor, the International Monetary Fund.

In the absence of an international insolvency process, it is not possible to draw a line under these debts and bring them to an end. Insolvency is effectively declared when the IMF is invited in. But in these cases insolvency does not mean release from the debts.

The IMF as creditor, and as the agent of all creditors, is not independent. Nevertheless in the context of insolvency the IMF plays the quasi-legal role of receiver, and decides on rates of repayment, conditions for repayment and whether new loans should be disbursed. Acting in the interest of creditors, the IMF is deeply reluctant to cancel debts. Instead its highly qualified staff protect creditors from carrying the burden of debt, and transfer this burden to the poorest people in debtor nations – those who have least responsibility for the crisis.

We in the international Jubilee 2000 movement regard this as a form of bondage by Western creditors – of whole peoples. In just the same way were the people of Israel held in bondage by the Pharaohs of Egypt. As long as the poorest countries are held in debt bondage, there can be no reason for obeying just one element of the Jubilee laws: the injunction to celebrate. More important (as we see it) are the injunctions first to cancel debts, free slaves and restore the land to its rightful owners. For, as the rock star Bono of U2 argues: 'Without a real commitment to debt relief, all New Year's Eve '99 will amount to is an updrawbridge scenario, a fancy dress ball at the castle where we (in the North) all play Louis XIV pissing across a moat of champagne on the poor ...'

The Jubilee 2000 vision is about restoring a moral dimension to economic relationships. But it is also about sound economics. About *periodically* correcting the fundamental injustice in relations between rich and poor, between debtors and creditors, between North and South. About imposing discipline and limitations on international capital flows, in particular lending and borrowing – so that public and private loans are disbursed or borrowed in a responsible, transparent and accountable way.

The Jubilee 2000 vision is about limitations on consumption

on the one hand, and renewal, growth and opportunity on the other. The Jubilee laws sought to limit exploitation and consumption. They set out to discipline the rich and the powerful, but also those who borrowed, who would not so easily be granted new loans. These laws were intended to curtail greed; to provide a disciplined framework for everyone to work within; and to give every person a chance for renewal, a fresh start.

In *Life after Debt* Michael Northcott draws deeply on the theological and ethical wellsprings of this vision in the Hebrew and Christian traditions, and in the stories and responses of the peoples of the South. He provides map and compass, encyclopaedia and guidebook for the Jubilee 2000 visionary and campaigner. I urge you to read it closely, to make good use of the carefully researched analyses and arguments, and to respect the voices of the South that speak through it.

ANN PETTIFOR

1 The Great Debt Disaster

Jeremy's Loan Trip to Kenya

It was my first time in Nairobi, a name which I gathered from the in-flight magazine means 'stream of cold water' in Maasai. Nairobi was built in the 1890s as a railhead for the Uganda Mombasa railway in a valley which belonged to the Maasai. Now in 1974 it is a bustling city, the largest in Africa between Egypt and Johannesburg, and provides the African base of the United Nations. I checked into the Fairview Hotel which is on Nairobi Hill, across from Uhuru Park. My room had a wonderful view across the treetops to the white and grey towers which are emerging in downtown Nairobi, some of them still surrounded by construction workers' scaffolding. I also had a view to the hills which surround this highland city on three sides. My meeting with the Finance Minister was not scheduled until the next day so I had plenty of time to check out the centre of the city.

I decided to walk down the hill into town after sitting so long in the plane. I was first struck by the smells and colours of bougainvillaea which dominate the outdoor reception area of the hotel, and are also much in evidence in the glorious space of Nairobi's City Park. The noise, speed and apparent chaos of the traffic also hit me. The most prominent vehicles were the minibuses, called *matutus*, painted in myriad colours and with bright slogans on the side, their drivers apparently competing both for the number of people they take on board and in the recklessness of their driving. I wandered into the bazaar next to the city market. The bright colours of the gaily printed clothes of the women sellers were so striking; and I could not resist the ornamental teak elephant family I found on one of the stalls, it was so delicately carved.

My first formal engagement was for dinner with two people from the British High Commission who were able to brief me about the government and its financial situation. The Prime Minister, Jomo Kenyatta, was popular with his people, and he planned a number of new projects which would include tourist developments and improvements in the national park, and horticultural developments to provide flowers and exotic fruits for export. The government was also wanting loans for road building and bridges, a new hospital and some infrastructure developments in the city centre.

That night, my first in Africa, I reflected on my assignment. I worked for one of the big four London clearing banks, and I had been commissioned as the Central and East Africa loans officer with a large lending target of £120 million. The sums involved were incredible, especially compared to the paltry amounts I had argued over lending to small businessmen at the high street branch in St Albans where I was seconded for a few months earlier in my career. These large sums of money were slices of the billions of petrodollars which were being deposited in the City of London as a result of the OPEC oil price rises in 1973. The bank could not keep so much money sitting underutilized in London, especially as interest rates were so low. It had to be lent out, and quickly, for us to pay returns to our depositors. My bosses reckoned that lending to developing countries made excellent sense. While small businessmen in St Albans could go bankrupt, countries and national governments could not.

The more stable of the newly independent African countries were good places to put some of our massive petrodollar deposits to work. Of course I could not lend all of my lending target on one visit, but the bank were also offering attractive bonuses for securing these loans and identifying suitable projects before year-end. Kenya seemed the ideal place to start. A peaceful country, the most stable in Africa I was told, its city centre seemed to be thriving and its agricultural and tourist industries were apparently ripe for development investment. They should provide a secure payback on the loans, as should the government which was apparently one of the least corrupt in Africa.

My meeting at the Finance Ministry went well. The Deputy Minister had been recently appointed and it turned out he had got his Ph.D. in economics from the LSE where I too had studied as an undergraduate. We had never actually met before but found we had friends in common, and as we chatted over coffee we reminisced about the heady days of sit-ins and student demos in Gower Street in the late 1960s. We discussed the programme of loans the government were seeking, the extent of their existing borrowings, and the projects for which the loans were intended.

After a morning's work we were driven to lunch in a grand tea-plantation house used by the government for entertaining foreign dignitaries in the oldest suburb of the city. In the afternoon we visited some of the sites of the intended development projects. We met engineers and architects, most of them from London-based firms, and saw plans for infrastructural developments, including roads, bridges, power stations and electric grids, and some of the sites where earthworks had already begun. We then went out to a large farm where the owner was planning a shift from maize cultivation into flowers and exotic fruits for export in partnership with a government agricultural agency.

In all on that one visit I managed to secure agreements to lend £24 million over three years. I was very pleased, as I had met more than 20 per cent of my lending target in only one visit. We are able to charge substantial fees for loans to governments, much larger than for loans to companies, so even before interest payments commence, our balance books show a good return on a deal like this. My Kenyan partners were also happy. With such low interest rates it was easy money and enabled the Prime Minister to fund a number of projects which, as well as helping the economic development of the country, would no doubt help maintain his popular standing at the next election. After a great visit to a wildlife park north of Nairobi, courtesy of the Finance Ministry, I returned to London with a satisfying sense of a mission accomplished which would benefit the bank and, I hoped, the people of Kenya.

The Origins of the Great Debt Disaster

It is possible to identify at least three principal causes of the great debt disaster. First was the excess liquidity in banks in the North generated by the collective action of the oil-producing states in raising oil prices in 1973. Many hoped that the OPEC action would presage a shift in the balance of power between the developed nations of the North and the newly independent nations of the South. If oil producers could charge more for their raw material, then so too perhaps could coffee producers, tin producers, or timber producers. But things did not work out like that. Increased oil prices, in 1973 and again in 1979, led to inflation and recession in the North. The capital flows generated were larger than the oil-producing countries could absorb and much of them ended up in London, Frankfurt, Paris and New York as deposits in search of borrowers. With a recession in the North, the obvious place to lend the money was in the developing economies of the newly independent countries of Asia, Africa and Latin America.

The second cause of the expansion of developing country debt in the 1970s was a move away from grant aid to developing nations in the South, and a growing preference for development loans from multilateral agencies such as the World Bank to new post-colonial governments (Corbridge, 1993).

The third major cause was the international deregulation of finance and banking which was driven by the growing transnationalization of banking and capital investment in the 1970s (Duchrow, 1995). Restrictions on the expansion of credit and loans by commercial banks were gradually removed in the 1970s and 1980s by governments in the North. The deregulation of the private creation of banking credits had the effect of privatizing the supply of money which in turn allowed for a massive global expansion in credit, and consequently in the amount of money in circulation around the world. Financial deregulation enhanced the flow of money from Western commercial banks to the economies of the South, most of which was in the form of loans to governments, rather than private investment capital (Corbridge, 1993). Deregulation also contributed to the development of what is sometimes called 'casino capitalism'. Large quantities of money became available for use in unproductive, highly risky, but potentially very profitable activities such as currency speculation, hedge funds and futures trading (Dodd, 1994). These activities in turn had disastrous consequences for many economies in the South which were over-borrowed, or whose currencies or primary commodities were traded down by speculators in the North.

The largest single lender to governments in Latin America, Asia and sub-Saharan Africa throughout the expansion of Western development lending in the 1970s and 1980s was the World Bank. But despite being the primary channel of official government lending from the North to the South, the Bank has a very poor record of assessing the viability and benefits of development projects for which it lends money. Loans officers like Jeremy were deployed by the Bank, and by commercial lenders, and their primary responsibility was to lend a certain amount of money. Many of these officers were not development experts and they tended to favour big capital-intensive projects because large amounts of money could be lent on one project, saving the time and money which establishing a portfolio of loans for smaller development projects would involve.

Many of the World Bank's most capital-intensive development projects were in fact disasters for the peoples and environments where the borrowed money was 'invested'. One such disaster is the resettlement scheme in northern Brazil known as Polonoroeste. Land in Brazil, as in many Latin American countries, is mostly owned by a very small number of families and companies. Extreme land inequality forces millions of people to eke out a subsistence from marginal lands such as steep hillsides or else to migrate to the already dreadfully overcrowded shanty towns of the cities. In order to relieve the problems of landlessness and hunger the World Bank funded a relocation programme which involved the building of a highway into the heart of the Amazon rainforest in the northwest province of Rondônia (Hancock, 1991). Settlers were encouraged to migrate along this road and to establish slash-and-burn farms in the tropical rainforest. The resultant damage to the Amazon forest has been catastrophic. The poor rainforest soil, once denuded of tree cover, soon loses its initial fertility and settlers have then to move on and destroy yet more forest. The main effect of the project has been to relieve the social and political pressure on rich landowners in parts of central Brazil, deferring the problem of land inequality to future generations at the cost of terrible environmental destruction (Hancock, 1991). Between 1982 and 1985 the World Bank lent $434.3 million for this one resettlement project.

The World Bank has also funded resettlement projects in Indonesia. Thus farmers from Java were resettled in Kalimantan and other heavily forested parts of the Indonesian archipelago, under an ongoing resettlement programme. In 1996 forest fires started by settlers, and also by logging companies, caused such environmental damage that the whole of the South-East Asian region was shrouded in a thick smog. The smog had devastating effects on the health of people in the region, and was one of the contributory factors in the region's economic crash in 1996–7. The Bank lent $600 million in the early stages of this disastrous resettlement programme.

In addition to resettlement programmes, the World Bank also had a penchant for big hydroelectric dams, despite the growing evidence of their disastrous human and environmental impacts. The series of thirty dams currently being constructed by the Indian government on the Narmada River will lead to the displacement of 1.5 million people, mostly of tribal or minority origin. Scientists believe that water-borne diseases will greatly increase throughout the region as a consequence of the project and they have also questioned the long-term viability of the hydroelectric and irrigation schemes associated with the dams (Hancock, 1991). But the Bank poured hundreds of millions of dollars into Narmada. It only began to reduce its commitment of funds in the early 1990s after considerable international pressure from non-governmental organizations and official aid agencies.

Officially sponsored and aided industrial and agricultural projects were also often misconceived, and frequently left the country with a scheme of such complexity and high running costs as to be unsustainable beyond the period of the loan. Richard Lombardi gives the example of a development project in Togo, one of the poorest countries in Africa:

> West Germany finances an important steel complex near Lomé, Togo's capital. On completion, the Togolese government realizes that no iron ore nor scrap metals are available for start-up. The credibility of Togo's head of state is in jeopardy. German technicians quickly dismantle an iron pier located at the port. Ironically, the pier had been constructed by Germany prior to World War I and was still functional and functioning. The steel mill closed down its operations when pig iron from the pier was exhausted. (George, 1988)

Graham Hancock describes the construction of a large fish farm in Egypt in unstable clay soil. The water in the ponds turned to liquid mud and most of the fish died (Hancock, 1991). Despite this the Food and Agriculture Organization of the United Nations – another though much smaller conduit of development loans and grants from North to South – continued to fund the project. Ironically a few miles away local smallholders had built a substantial fish farm on the shores of a lake where the land was naturally more suited to hydroculture. Their farm produced 27,000 tons of fish a year without any help from Western development experts or loans (Hancock, 1991).

In addition to questionable development projects, much of the increased lending to developing countries in the 1970s and 1980s went to fuel an arms race which reflected superpower rivalry for geopolitical influence between the Western powers, and especially between the USA and the Soviet bloc countries. Thus in one year, 1983, governments in sub-Saharan Africa together spent $2.2 billion on imported military hardware and only $1.7 billion on health (Cheru, 1989). In many indebted developing countries in the late 1970s and early 1980s the proportion of debt spent on the military was in excess of 20 per cent, and in some equivalent to 40 per cent of the external debt (Cheru, 1989). Between them twenty-five African countries who had to renegotiate debt in the 1980s had spent $11 billion on weapons. Frequently these weapons were then used against the citizens of these countries, as corrupt dictators sought to hold on to power and suppress popular efforts to install more representative and honest rulers (Cheru, 1989).

A common feature of the corruption which militarization sustained was the kleptocracy practised by the dictators and prime ministers who sponsored it. Much of the money lent never actually left the West. Dictators in South America, Africa and Asia were (and some still are) notorious for their corrupt abuse of public finances. Many of these dictators, such as Ferdinand Marcos in the Philippines or Jean-Claude (Baby Doc) Duvalier in Haiti, contracted debts on behalf of the people they ruled which were then used to enhance their own personal wealth. Western lenders turned a blind eye to these practices, however, as loans were often a means of propping up dictators who, though corrupt and unpopular in their own countries, were seen as allies of Western interests against the perceived global threat from Soviet and Chinese-sponsored communism. As a result much external debt from the South ended up in bank accounts in the North, frequently in the secretive banks of Switzerland, or in offshore banking zones such as the Cayman Islands. It also funded the purchase of country houses or city-centre properties in Europe and North America; properties which were not only useful on overseas trips, but would also provide refuges for deposed dictators and their families when their people, or more often their well-funded armies, turned against them.

Of course not all loans were embezzled or used for disastrous prestige projects or military spending. In countries with more representative governments and stricter budgetary controls a good proportion of the loans helped in the building of infrastructure projects such as roads and power lines. Kenya used development loans for just such purposes, as the opening story illustrates. But even where loans were used for purposes that improved the infrastructure of the country, the poor often experienced no real benefit. Poor people without access to electricity derive little benefit from hydroelectric schemes built on their former tribal lands. The poor have little use for metalled highways designed for the private cars and trucks of city dwellers and traders. They have no use at all for the cut flowers (and associated pesticides and herbicides) grown on former agricultural land for Western florists.

Though they did not reap the benefits of debt in the short term, in the long term it has been the poor and their children who have suffered most from the debt burden. As interest rates have risen and the terms of trade have worsened, the costs of debt servicing and repayment have risen inexorably. Kenya today has an external debt of $6.7 billion, or roughly $1,100 for every man, woman and child in Kenya. Debt repayments are crippling the still predominantly agricultural economy of Kenya. As more and more land is converted from staple crops like maize to export crops such as mangetout, haricot beans and other air-flown produce sold in Northern supermarkets, the poor increasingly suffer from hunger and poor nutrition in the villages of rural Kenya and in the shanty towns of Nairobi.

In addition to official lending by intergovernmental agencies such as the World Bank, an increasing share of lending was taken up by syndicates of international banks such as the four London clearing-house banks, especially Midland and Barclays, and American banks such as Citicorp and Chase Manhattan. These large multinational financial organizations often lent many times more in credits than they held in deposits. As we have seen, banks were able to do this because of the inter-nationalization and deregulation of the banking system in the 1970s. This meant that banks no longer had to keep a certain proportion of their loans as reserves. Instead they could lend what the loan market could stand (Corbridge, 1993). As a consequence commercial lending and debt, including national, corporate and personal debt, have increased exponentially in the last thirty years. Loans to governments in the South were considered good risks because countries didn't go bankrupt. These loans are also highly profitable because banks charge very high fees in negotiating loans to governments. And though they are negotiated by loans officers from one specific bank, the risks are shared by loan syndication with other banks.

In a deregulated financial system the quantity of money in circulation is no longer limited by the amounts of money physically minted and printed by national government banks. National banks have therefore to resort to new measures to control the private supply of money. As a consequence interest rates rose in the early 1980s in order to control the inflationary expansion of the newly commercialized money supply in deregulated Western banking systems. With these higher rates of interest, which doubled between the late 1970s and early 1980s, developing countries found it impossible to find enough foreign exchange to pay the increased interest payments on their external debts to the banks of the North.

The first nation to default on its loans was Zaire in 1975. Between 1979 and 1982, twenty-three nations had to renegotiate their loans with their creditors. But it was not until the government of Mexico declared that it could no longer meet its loan commitments in August 1982 that the world really awoke to the potential scale of the debt crisis (Corbridge, 1993). To resolve the crisis, the USA increased International Monetary Fund quotas to fund a new debt management strategy. US government agencies also advanced foreign exchange to Mexico against future revenues from oil and agricultural exports and the International Monetary Fund forced the more than one thousand commercial banks with loans to Mexico to advance a further 7 per cent of the value of their loans in return for a debt rescheduling package designed to allow the loans to be serviced and eventually repaid (Corbridge, 1993).

To prevent other indebted countries from defaulting on their debts the International Monetary Fund and the World Bank began to advance stand-by loans to countries in difficulties. The new monies went direct to private banks to meet interest payments of debtor nations on condition that they submitted their national budgets to financial austerity packages.

This strategy was not altruistic but was designed to shore up the Western banking system which could have been undermined by the extent of its exposure to developing-country debt. It was also designed to ensure that in the new global financial order nations would not be allowed to file for bankruptcy. A significant implication of the bailout mechanisms provided by the International Monetary Fund is that they have underwritten unwise banking behaviour on the part of both official agencies and commercial lenders (Dodd, 1994). This consequence is sometimes referred to as 'moral hazard': by rewarding excessive and risky lending, Western governments and international financial institutions were in effect telling Western bankers that they could go on lending money irresponsibly and when they got into difficulties arrangements would be made to bail them out.

Both the International Monetary Fund and the World Bank have their origins in the conference which was held at Bretton Woods in the shadow of Mount Washington in New Hampshire, USA, towards the end of the Second World War. The International Bank for Reconstruction and Development, commonly known as the World Bank, was established primarily in order to lend funds for the reconstruction of Europe after the war (Duchrow, 1995). At this conference the English economist John Maynard Keynes urged a powerful case for money, mostly American money, to be lent to Europe in order to regenerate the global trading and financial environment on which the United States also depended for its economic prospects (Buchan, 1997). Under what came to be known as the Marshall Plan, the United States provided $17 billion in loans and gift aid to Western Europe between 1947 and 1952 to rescue and rebuild the damaged economies of the region. The Marshall Plan anticipated and enabled the growth of development aid not only to Europe but also to developing countries. The Marshall Plan was also a global embodiment of key elements of Keynesian orthodoxy.

Keynes argued that when national economies are depressed (or underdeveloped) governments should borrow money in order to finance public works and generate employment. He envisaged public borrowing as economic pump-priming that would generate increased economic activity. This in turn would enhance tax receipts, allowing governments in better times to pay off the debt. Inflation also figured in his theory, for Keynes reckoned that increased government borrowing would drive down the real value of money, thus in turn reducing the actual value of the debt which started the virtuous cycle in the first place. Keynes' theory turned the historic vice of warring monarchs and despots (funding their wars through debt) into a modern virtue: debt, or public debt at any rate, is good for the economy, and therefore good for society.

Post-war governments in Europe consequently borrowed vast sums of money to fund reconstruction. Much of this money was in the form of government bonds though some was borrowed from private banks, most notably in Canada. Some took the form of external debt, borrowed from overseas corporations and institutions, just like the debt of developing countries in the South today. The mountain of money involved in the Marshall Plan, some of which was donated and some of which was loaned, helped to rebuild the social fabric of Europe after the war. But it also funded the militarization of international relations – the Cold War – which followed the carving-up of Europe after the Second World War. Government borrowings were utilized to build the vast nuclear arms stockpiles that accumulated in Eastern and Western Europe and North America from the 1950s to the 1980s. This period also established a pattern in which governments regularly spend more than they receive in taxes, and a legacy of permanent national debt whose accumulating interest is a deferred tax which will fall on future generations.

Keynes' theory of debt was a powerful, though deeply flawed, theory. It helped to create a world in which governments would come to regard rising levels of consumer debt as a positive economic indicator, and in which the richest nation on earth, the USA, now has a national debt exceeding $3 trillion (as a consequence primarily of profligate spending on military hardware). But whereas the USA is able to sustain a high standard of living for many of its citizens while maintaining this vast debt, through a combination of internal economic resilience and international influence, backed by military power, the same cannot be said for debtor countries in the South.

The combined external debt owed by the governments of all debtor countries in sub-Saharan Africa stood in 1997 at $196 billion according to figures from the Organization for Economic Co-operation and Development (OECD, 1998). The enormity of the debt of these poor countries has led to the virtual enslavement of their peoples to debt repayments. In many countries in the region these repayments exceed 50 per cent of national income. In Mozambique, where three out of five adults are illiterate, debt repayments take up 90 per cent of export revenues. As a consequence Mozambique, the poorest country on earth, exported $113 million in 1997 to the banks and governments of the rich North. Annually poor indebted countries in the South export over $200 billion to the rich North in debt service payments including interest and capital repayments (OECD, 1998).

To make debt repayments on this scale, monies are diverted from education, housing, and public health programmes, including clean water and sewerage systems, vaccination programmes and the building of hospitals and clinics. More and more land is diverted from the production of staple foods to the cultivation of export crops – including tea, coffee, exotic fruits and flowers – which earn foreign exchange for debt repayment, instead of food crops for domestic consumption.

Environments are also despoiled to help repay debt. In Central Africa, as in the Amazon, vast areas of irreplaceable tropical forest are being cut down to meet debt repayments, and to provide land for peasant farmers shifted from ancestral lands which are taken over for commercial and export-oriented farming. Seas and rivers are exploited unsustainably for prawn and fish farming, and for industrial fishing which often destroys fishing grounds for local subsistence fishing communities. And because so many countries have been instructed by the World Bank and the International Monetary Fund to increase production for export, the price of many raw materials and primary agricultural commodities has been going down on world markets since the 1970s as a consequence of oversupply.

The human and environmental costs of the great debt disaster have been incalculable. One consequence has been a global redistribution of income from poor to rich countries. Since 1970 the gap between the richest fifth and the poorest fifth of the world has doubled. The scale of debt servicing means that the South now exports more capital to the North than it receives back from the North in aid, loans, inward private investment and export earnings.

The United Nations Children's Fund estimates that in one year alone, 1988, half a million children died because of the burden of debt interest and repayment (Jolly, 1989): from the mid-1980s to the late 1990s the figure amounts to tens of millions dead. Children die from preventable diseases, from malnutrition, or through drinking contaminated water; some die at birth, and in sub-Saharan Africa one in twenty of their mothers dies in childbirth as well. As Professor Adebayo Adedeji, the former Executive Secretary of the UN Economic Commission for Africa, puts it:

> So severe has been the exacerbating burden of debt on the ordinary people in the debt-distressed countries that their destructive impact is comparable only to that of war, the only difference being that it is children rather than soldiers who are dying and instead of millions wounded, there are millions unemployed. The war-like impact of debt is tearing down schools, hospitals and rending the fabric of societies. (World Development Movement, 1996)

From reading Western newspapers or watching Western televisions, few would have made the connection between the tragic genocide in Rwanda in 1993 and the great debt disaster. Rwanda, like all sub-Saharan Africa, has a big external debt – latest estimate $1,041 million – and in 1992 took orders from the International Monetary Fund and the World Bank to increase the price of basic foodstuffs and reduce public spending in order to divert more revenues to external debt repayments. Conditions were made worse by the dramatic drop in the price of coffee on world markets in 1992 because of oversupply by so many indebted coffee-producing nations. The resultant impoverishment of the Rwandan people exacerbated pre-existent ethnic tensions and dissatisfaction with the government. In a bid to hold on to power the government actively whipped up ethnic tension through officially controlled radio and television networks, a strategy which escalated into genocide, and which the world's media blamed on African tribalism. Rwanda may be the worst example, but the debt crisis has contributed to political and civil unrest in many indebted poor countries and it is a significant causal factor in the more than fifty 'low level conflicts' currently under way in Africa, Asia and Latin America.

The Bondage of Debt and the Redeeming Jubilee

During his brief three-year ministry, Jesus Christ spoke often of debt and debt forgiveness. The economic situation in first-century Palestine was determined by the growing power of the Roman Empire over the Jewish people and their lands. Pressure to pay taxes, imposed to support the vast armies and bureaucracies of Empire, was driving many Jewish farmers into debt. In lieu of unpayable debt many of them had to hand over their land to their creditors. The loss of their land reduced farmers to wage labourers and to the status of sub-citizens as membership of the people of Israel was traditionally linked to landholding, and the subsistence economy of the first century still revolved around the family farm.

Jesus himself highlights the injustice of this situation in his parable of the Labourers in the Vineyard (Matthew 20.1–16). The landowner is said to have been shocked when he encountered unemployed labourers in the market place at the end of the day and to correct this injustice he hired them and offered them a full day's pay, even though only one working hour was left in the day.

Recent archaeological finds indicate that the influence of Empire on Palestine was not only driving small farmers into debt and landlessness, but also encouraging the creation of large agricultural and trading concerns. The remains of large wine and olive presses, and of bunkhouses suitable for large groups of farm workers to sleep in, have been found on sites south of Galilee. Archaeologists have also uncovered evidence of fish drying and fish bottling facilities in the region of Tyre, the deep Mediterranean seaport, where products such as fish paste, olive oil and wine would have been exported to Rome (Freyne, 1995).

While the Empire generated new forms of international trade, its taxation and trading regimens drove many peasants into landlessness, penury and debt slavery. But the development of trade created a new class of wealthy urban people who lived in some luxury while imposing taxes and tithes on the increasingly impoverished rural smallholders which pressed them further into debt.

Seen in this light, the first words which Jesus is reported as uttering in his public ministry, in the synagogue at Capernaum, take on tremendous significance. His address on the Sabbath, in the town which frequently gave him a roof over his head, began with a reading from Isaiah in which the prophet announces good news to the poor and 'the year of the Lord's favour' (Luke 4.18–19). At the end of the reading Jesus rolled up the scroll and announced to all who were listening to him that 'today this scripture has been fulfilled in your hearing' (Luke 4.21). The year of the Lord's favour is a clear reference to the Jubilee, the fiftieth year, when all debts in Israel were to be cancelled and lands and houses lost through debt were to be restored to their original owners (Leviticus 25). By commencing his ministry with a reference to Jubilee, Jesus brings one of the central strands of socio-economic law in the Hebrew Bible into direct connection with the new society, the kingdom of God, which he announces has come in his person.

In the Hebrew Bible the concept and practice of Jubilee is strongly connected to the experience of Exodus when Yahweh released the Hebrews from slavery in Egypt. The Joseph narratives describe how as a consequence of a great famine which affected Egypt and its neighbours, all the people of the region were drawn into a feudal relationship with Pharaoh who, because of Joseph's visionary stewardship, had stores of food and seed to give famine-stricken farmers. However, in exchange for seed the farmers gave up their rights over their lands to Pharaoh and became in effect feudal tenants who farmed the land on his behalf and gave a proportion of their farm produce to Pharaoh every year as rent (Genesis 47). Landlessness soon led to slavery, and from their condition of bondage the Israelites cried to the Lord and were liberated from Egypt and ultimately entered the Promised Land.

When they came into the land to possess it, the Israelites heard or rehearsed constant reminders – in their rituals and festivals, in their laws and in the utterances of their prophets – that they enjoyed the land as gift. They were exhorted not to take their possession of the land for granted for it was really God's and not theirs: 'the earth is the Lord's and all that is in it' (Psalm 24.1). The land was gifted to them to tend and to inhabit, but the consequent rights to land of every Israelite family were balanced by the ultimate right of the Lord as the true landowner: 'The land shall not be sold in perpetuity, for the land is mine; with me you are but aliens and tenants' (Leviticus 25.23).

The Jubilee regulations in Leviticus provided a range of mechanisms which limited the sale of land, and ensured its continuing fair distribution between all the families of Israel, mechanisms which provided 'for the redemption of the land' (Leviticus 25.24). When a farmer got into debt, through a bad harvest or poor farming practices, the law provided that the farmer's nearest relative should have first right of purchase of the portion of the land that had to be sold to pay off the debt (Leviticus 25.25). If a person had to sell all their land to get out of debt then it was the responsibility of their next of kin to provide employment for them and to give them interest-free loans (Leviticus 25.35). Usury, the lending of money at interest, was forbidden in Israelite society because it would bind the debtors to debt bondage which would have exacerbated their landless condition, contrary to the redemptive intent of Yahweh in saving their ancestors from landlessness and debt bondage (Wright, 1990).

Even with these provisions, it was still the case that some people found themselves both landless and with unpayable money debts. In such cases the law prescribed that they should not become another person's slave but rather their dependent labourers (Leviticus 25.35). Dependent labourers were not, though, true citizens in Israelite society. The Jubilee law was instituted so that every fifty years lands and houses which had been lost to their original owners through poverty and debt were to be restored to them or their descendants: 'if there are not sufficient means to recover it, what was sold shall remain with the purchaser until the year of jubilee; in the jubilee it shall be released, and the property shall be returned' (Leviticus 25.28).

These redemption and Jubilee regulations were designed to do a number of things. They kept land holdings within wider kinship groups. They prevented one kinship group from acquiring too much land and they ensured the continuation of smaller family land holdings with the periodic fifty-year redistribution. This Jubilee redistribution meant that succeeding generations did not suffer forever from the misfortunes of their parents or grandparents. The regulations were also designed to minimize the impact of debt and debt bondage on the people of Israel. And finally they ensured that the natural resources of the people of Israel would be fairly distributed, and inequality limited, from one generation to the next.

It is sometimes said that the Jubilee regulations were impractical and that they were never practised in Israel. Some scholars argue that they were a utopian invention by exiled Israelites in Babylon who looked back and invented such laws as would have prevented the kind of injustices which led to internal divisions, and eventually exile, in earlier generations. But Christopher Wright points out that the Jubilee laws clearly reflect the earliest religious traditions of the Israelites which linked the redemption of Yahweh and the gift of the Land to particular socio-economic arrangements, and that they there-fore do reflect socio-economic practice in ancient Israel (Wright, 1990). The Jubilee links Israel's earliest religious sense of Yahweh's ownership of the land to the rights of every Israelite family to economic self-sufficiency, based on the inalienability of their landholding.

The concept of Jubilee is closely linked to another Israelite law concerning land and its possession which was the Sabbath of the land: 'in the seventh year there shall be a sabbath of complete rest for the land, a sabbath for the Lord: you shall not sow your field or prune your vineyard' (Leviticus 25.4). The Sabbath of the land seems to have had three distinct purposes. One reflects the idea that natural resources and animals have their limits. They should not be relentlessly pressed into the service of human need, and especially not of human greed. A fallow year ensured that the land had a rest and would have helped to prevent erosion and desertification, to which the fragile lands of the Ancient Near East were and are particularly prone (Northcott, 1996).

The second purpose was to set human work and creativity within certain limits. In contrast to the unceasing demands on human life generated by modern factories, shops and markets which function seven days a week, and by the continual accumulation of interest and monetary value in modern banking systems (which recognize no sabbath break), the laws of Sabbath and Jubilee required rest (for people and nature) in the economy of Israel. In this way economic processes were prevented from attaining supremacy over human life.

Third, the fallow year had a function in relation to justice and the poor. In the seventh year the landless poor were to be allowed to gather food from those fields, vineyards and olive groves which were left fallow and unharvested by their owners (Exodus 23.10–11). According to the Deuteronomic law, the seventh year also provided an opportunity for the release of debts and slaves, as well as the release of the land (Deuteronomy 15.1–3).

As with Jubilee, the Sabbath laws were designed to enshrine in law the fact that sharing in God's divine ownership of creation carries with it considerable obligations: to the land itself, to kin, to neighbours and to resident aliens. The Sabbath laws like the Jubilee laws were designed to prevent impoverishment, debt bondage and slavery from becoming predominant features of Israelite society.

The Sabbath laws find their ultimate meaning in their connection with the Sabbath of the Lord. Yahweh is said to have rested on the seventh day of creation and to have prescribed a day of rest every seventh day for the people of Israel. On the seventh day the people of Israel were to rest from their work, and to turn their attention to the worship of the Lord. The hallowed day of the Sabbath, and the Sabbath year, prevented work from becoming the dominant activity of ancient Israelites, and prescribed limits to wealth creation. The Sabbath redirected the Israelites to the true source of their wealth and fulfilment – to the Lord, who had provided them with the abundance of creation for their enjoyment and security, whose righteousness and justice required that they continue to share its abundance fairly and equally with one another.

Worship of Yahweh in Israel was rooted in the affirmation of the sovereignty of Yahweh over creation and over human society, a sovereignty that set limits on human power and human ownership. Where human social structures created great inequality, debt bondage and slavery, the religiously based laws of Jubilee and Sabbath were designed to reconnect the socio-economic system of Israelite society with the worship of this sovereign God who was the same God who redeemed the people of Israel from slavery, and who continued to require the redemption of the poor, the widow, the alien and the fatherless.

What are the implications of Jubilee and Sabbath law for the current debt crisis? The debt crisis is a tragic consequence of what happens when money and trading systems are given authority in human legal systems above divinely instituted moral laws, and where in consequence money, and particularly its corporate purveyors, acquire rights, as legal but fictive persons, which subvert the human rights of actual persons. That children die in order that their governments can make debt repayments to rich nations and bankers is the clearest indicator of what happens when humans ascribe authority to that which has no true right or claim to such authority over them.

In medieval Europe the principles and values enshrined in the Jubilee and Sabbath laws in ancient Israel were adopted in modified form by the ancient Christian Church. Efforts were made to submit the authority of princes, and the power of money, to the prior claims of divine law and authority. As a consequence, until the late Middle Ages the lending of money for interest was restricted and controlled under both ecclesiastical and common law. Economic activity was also forbidden on Sundays. And ecclesiastical lawyers recognized that when a poor person had to steal from the rich in order to feed and clothe himself and his family, then this was not theft but a moral necessity as God's original ordering of the world was intended to provide for all, and not just a few. In this and many other ways the Church traditionally taught that property ownership carried duties as well as rights and that there are moral limits to wealth inequality.

Most modern Christians no longer eschew usury in the way their forebears did. In the West many use credit cards, purchase houses through mortgages, and save for retirement through pension funds which, among other activities, put money into interest-bearing bank deposits, or bonds and gilts in order to achieve growth which keeps pace with or outpaces inflation. Christian principles of generosity and debt forgiveness no longer act as controls on commercial lending and borrowing. However, it remains the case that these ancient Jewish and Christian ideals still inform most Western legal and economic systems in the form of bankruptcy provision for individuals and firms which have – through foolishness, poor judgement or bad luck – contracted debts which are beyond their means to repay. A person who is declared bankrupt loses much of what he owns, though liquidators usually allow him to keep a roof over his head, house furnishings, clothes and personal necessities and possibly a private car. But once the liquidators are finished, the person's outstanding debts are cancelled, forgiven, and they may in time contract new loans and commence new businesses.

However, in the case of international debt the bankruptcy route has not been permitted to countries such as Zaire, Mexico,

Nigeria, Peru and Indonesia, who threatened to default on their external debt. Much of the old and unpayable debt is now in the hands of Western governments and of international financial institutions such as the International Monetary Fund and the World Bank. Various schemes for debt remission have been proposed by Western creditor governments, who are also the governors of these institutions. But the conditions applying to all such schemes, and their accounting mechanisms, mean that in reality only a very small proportion, less than 5 per cent, of the total of external debt of the poorest countries in the South has been forgiven. Consequently throughout the 1980s and 1990s in most cases the quantity of debt has increased (as unpaid interest is added to the principal of the loan). So too has the suffering of the peoples of indebted countries.

If Britain and Germany had been treated in this way by North American bankers after the Second World War, much of the reconstruction on which the current prosperity of Europe rests would never have taken place. Instead the Allies let Germany off hundreds of millions of dollars of what they judged to be unpayable debt in the 1950s, and Britain has also benefited from substantial debt relief, particularly from the USA, since the Second World War.

Christians have been prominent among those who have been calling and campaigning for the banks and governments of the North to forgive the unpayable debts of the poorest countries in the South. They argue that the laws of Jubilee and Sabbath are a significant biblical warrant for debt forgiveness and that the divine sovereignty over human work and economy which these laws sustained requires that money debts be set aside when human lives are endangered by them. The claim that human welfare should take priority over the laws of monetary exchange also reflects a growing recognition among Christians in both North and South of the moral evils which are fostered by modern economic systems when they are not directed to the common good by effective social regulation.

The mobilization of the biblical Jubilee in making the moral case for debt forgiveness has been powerfully advanced by the coalition of church and secular aid agencies which is known as

Jubilee 2000. The Jubilee 2000 Coalition has local organizations in forty-two countries around the world and they are campaigning for the equivalent of a Marshall Plan to be mobilized by the international financial institutions and the rich governments of the North to resolve the debt crisis by cancelling the debt overhang of unpayable debts contracted by the fifty-two poorest and most indebted countries. The Coalition argues that unpayable debts should be cancelled because they are in most cases odious debts. The concept of odious debt entered international law in a US Supreme Court judgement against Great Britain which was seeking in 1923 to challenge Costa Rican laws which repudiated debts contracted to the Royal Bank of Canada by a former dictator. The US Supreme Court Chief Justice William Howard Taft took the view that since the money had been lent for no 'legitimate use' its attempts to enforce repayment against the new and legitimate government of Costa Rica 'must fail' (Chomsky, 1998).

Most of the unpayable debts of the Jubilee 2000 list of indebted nations were contracted on behalf of dictators and their illegitimate governments, or by private companies, without the knowledge or consent of the people who are now having to repay these debts, and were not used for their benefit. For example the government of Nelson Mandela in South Africa is paying annual interest and loan repayments of £2,300 million on debts of more than £11 billion which were contracted by the former apartheid regime in its war against its own people, and the other nations of Southern Africa. The cost of repaying these odious debts is crippling the efforts of the new South Africa to improve the lot of its people.

The total cost of debt forgiveness for all of the countries on the Jubilee 2000 Coalition list is estimated at approximately $100 billion, which is around the cost of the Marshall Plan in the 1950s. Western financial institutions were able to find $25 billion to finance a rescue package for the economies of East Asia after the region's financial crash in 1997. However, there is a lack of international political will to fund similar solutions for the poorest nations, who are predominantly located in Africa. The West has considerable private and public economic investments in the East Asian economies and many East Asian companies are significant investors and employers in Western nations, including the UK.

Supporters of the Jubilee 2000 debt cancellation proposal argue that debt forgiveness is ultimately not about charity but about justice under international law. Odious debts should not be repaid by people who did not contract them and who did not benefit from them. Njongonkulu Ndungane, the Archbishop of Cape Town, argues that the concept of odious debt provides a legal basis on which debt forgiveness should be organized and he has proposed the establishment of an international mediation council to oversee the process of debt write-off. But the Archbishop also recognizes that law alone will not provide the motivation for debt forgiveness on the scale that is proposed. Ultimately it is a theological and moral as well as a legal challenge:

> We are at the doorstep of the next one thousand years in the history of humankind. The first Christians stood on the threshold of the first millennium in a state of hopelessness after the Crucifixion of Christ. But God raised him from the dead: hence our age is one of hope, an age of new beginnings, an age of the Resurrection faith. The opportunity to start anew must be seized. Through an act of immeasurable power and grace, let us reshape the world's economy. In this way the third millennium can be a Jubilee celebration, and the Risen Lord can help us understand his proclamation 'Behold I make all things new!' (Ndungane in Spray, 1997)

Sources

John Buchan (1997), *Frozen Desire: The Meaning of Money* (NY: Farrar, Straus and Giroux)

Fantu Cheru (1989), *The Silent Revolution: Debt, Development and Democracy* (London: Zed Books)

Noam Chomsky (1998), 'The people always pay' (London, *Guardian*, 12 May)

Stuart Corbridge (1993), *Debt and Development* (Oxford: Blackwell)

Nigel Dodd (1994), *The Sociology of Money* (New York: Continuum)

Ulrich Duchrow (1995), *Alternatives to Global Capitalism: Drawn from Biblical History, Designed for Political Action* (Eng. trans., Utrecht: International Books)

Sean Freyne (1995), 'Herodian Economics in Galilee: Searching for a Suitable Model' in Philip F. Esler (ed.), *Modelling Early Christianity: Social Scientific Studies of the New Testament in its Context* (London: Routledge)

Susan George (1988), *A Fate Worse Than Debt* (London: Penguin)

Graham Hancock (1991), *Lords of Poverty* (London: Mandarin)

Richard Jolly (1989), 'The Human Dimensions of International Debt' in Adrian Hewitt and Bowen Wells (eds.), *Growing Out of Debt: All Party Parliamentary Group on Overseas Development* (London: Overseas Development Institute)

Michael Northcott (1996), *The Environment and Christian Ethics* (Cambridge: Cambridge University Press)

OECD (1998), *External Debt Statistics: Resource Flows, Debt Stocks and Debt Service, 1986–1997* (OECD: Paris)

Bill Peters (1996), *Grass Roots Mobilisation for Debt Remission: The Jubilee 2000 Campaign* (London: Jubilee 2000)

Paul Spray (1997), *Change the DEBT Rules: A Basic Policy Paper* (London: Christian Aid)

World Development Movement (1996) *Debt: How the Poor are Paying the Rich* (London: World Development Movement)

Christopher J. H. Wright (1990), *God's People in God's Land: Family, Land and Property in the Hebrew Bible* (Exeter: Paternoster Press)

Organizations

Fuller details of the Jubilee 2000 Coalition campaign are described in Chapter 4. The coalition welcomes supporters and donations as it campaigns for international debt forgiveness. Its website describes a range of campaign actions which readers of this book may want to engage in:

Jubilee 2000 Coalition PO Box 100, London SE1 7RT
Tel: +44 (0) 171 401 9999 *Fax:* +44 (0) 171 401 3999
E-mail: mail@jubilee2000uk.org
Website: Jubilee 2000 http://www.jubilee2000uk.org/

2 Adjusted to Debt

Beatriz Mendoza's Education in Debt-Ridden Bolivia

I live in El Alto which is a large satellite city on the plain above
La Paz, the capital city of Bolivia. It is often very cold up here
as the winds blow straight off the snow-capped Andes. My
family came here more than ten years ago. My father was a
miner and lost his job when the government privatized the
silver mines in 1986. We heard of other people coming here
and when we first arrived we stayed with relatives while we got
a small patch of land and built our house, which is made from
adobe (dried mud).

El Alto has grown so much since we came because so many
people have been forced to leave the land and the mines
because of bad times. It is now almost as big as La Paz
though the area we live in is pretty rough compared to the
capital. The houses are very close together and the street is
just mud and gets very messed up when it rains. But at least
we have electricity and clean water after six years of pleas and
protests to the local government. The more recent arrivals in
the newest areas don't have them and open sewers run down
the middle of the mud streets where the children play, along
with the sheep and the goats their parents still try to keep.

I am nineteen and I have just finished school. Our school, the
oldest in El Alto, was the most rundown place you can imagine.
All the windows were broken, the roofs leaked, the classrooms
were full of puddles, the blackboards had holes in them. There
were around fifty or sixty of us in each class, we had to sit four
to a small bench and people still had to sit on windowsills or
stand at the back. Sometimes the rain or even snow would
come in and right on to your head and your school book so

your writing got smudged. Our parents protested to the authorities but they said there was no money to fix up the buildings. And there were five thousand children in this one rundown school, primary and secondary. The school ran in shifts, morning, afternoon, night-time; it was very chaotic.

The teaching was also very bad and it was hard to learn anything at all. The teachers hardly ever prepared their lessons, and they were always going on strike because they were not getting paid. Once our teacher refused to come into the classroom because he had not been paid. We were waiting for him but he refused until he got paid. But what about us? Mostly the teachers don't care, they just come for their allocated hours and then go to their other jobs, like taxi-driving. Lots of my classmates dropped out of school. Some of them got work and made more money than their parents and others joined violent gangs and got involved in crime and drugs.

The poor state of my school is nothing unusual in Bolivia. Public services are all very run down and not properly funded. It has been this way for years even though our country is quite rich in natural resources like gas and silver and fertile soil, and there are only seven million people and the country is quite large. The reason is that for decades governments have been borrowing lots of money from overseas and lining their own pockets. Now most of the money from taxes and from exports is going to pay the interest on the debt.

Also there are not enough jobs for our parents because the government sacked lots of its workers and the businesses in La Paz do not take on many people either. Often my father gets temporary work for a few days here and there at building sites or warehouses but nothing that lasts more than a week or two. My mother has been luckier. She got a job in a grocery store in La Paz and it has lasted more than a year now, though the wages they get between them are not enough to pay for heating, medicine, school uniform and the other things we need. My mother can sometimes bring home fresh fruit or bread which is no longer saleable in the shop and then we have a real feast. Mostly we live off maize meal and beans.

There are six children in my family and my youngest brother is only four and he is sick a lot. He is always getting bronchitis and needs a lot of medicine. The house is very damp because when it rains the mud bricks get quite wet as we did not have money for a proper concrete foundation and the tin roof is not very waterproof.

Things are no better in the rural areas. In fact friends who recently came from there say it is even worse. There are almost no teachers there, and it is hard to find jobs. The small farmers are all being swallowed up by big landowners and those that are left are growing mostly coca leaves which the government doesn't like and so it tries to stop them. The Americans have even sent soldiers into the hill farms and used chemicals to destroy the coca fields but we have been growing coca in Bolivia for thousands of years. Our old people use it and we use it as medicine; it is not just for drugs. The money they are using to destroy coca fields they could be spending on our schools and on paying our teachers so the youth of Bolivia could have some hope in the future.

You might be surprised but I am now attending the teacher training college in La Paz. I taught my younger sisters and brothers to read. I think it is the best thing I can do for my country: to teach better than our teachers taught us and give more hope to the younger people coming up. But the college is not so good either. It is on a big patch of land but the buildings are very small and grass grows up to your knees outside. Really the whole place looks completely abandoned. The teachers are also quite mixed. Some are very motivated and a few are well educated but a lot of them are not much further on than us and do not even have degrees. Like most of the other students I have to work as well as study so there is less time to protest and hold committees and try to make things better. We study in the mornings and I work in the afternoons in a store near where my mother works. She heard about a vacancy and my money helps to make ends meet.

The most hopeful thing I do is with a youth group called MUVESA, *Mundo Verde y Sano* (Green and Healthy World). We have been teaching children in the community about the environment and also arts and crafts and we play games with them – a little bit of everything! A non-governmental organization called Gregoria Apaza (a Christian Aid partner) gives us some materials and support. We have some great kids even though many of them actually run away from school to come to the group's activities. This is rather difficult. We don't really know their reasons. Are they just trying to get out of lessons at school or do they see us as a real opportunity where they can receive training and learn something? It's great working with the kids, especially out in the open air; it's very different from working in a classroom, there are no rules, no obligations. The children come because they want to, not because anyone is forcing them. The activities in the group are very different from their activities in the school which are restricted to academic subjects, here they learn to play, to be free.

Adjusting People and Structures for Debt Repayment

Bolivia has an external debt of $5,067 million, or $6,800 for every person in the country. After Peru, which owes $30,831 million, it is the most heavily indebted poor country in South America. For much of the 1980s and early 1990s the costs of servicing this debt absorbed more than half the country's annual income from exports. In 1997 Bolivia paid $334 million to American and European banks, and to international financial institutions, or 27 per cent of the total value of its export earnings. The two largest creditors are Japan ($1,504 million) and Germany ($491 million). In 1996 Britain, which has 4 per cent of Bolivia's external debt, received approximately $40 million in interest and capital repayments from Bolivia. Most of this transfer of funds from a poor to a rich country was to the Export Credits Guarantee Department of the British government's Department of Trade and Industry (Garrett, Hanlon and Pettifor, 1998). This Department acts as a guarantor to British exports to countries overseas. When countries default on payment for exports the Department pays British companies which have applied for a guarantee the money they would otherwise have lost. The Department also advances payment to companies that export to countries with a poor payment record. As this book was going to press Japan announced that it would forgive all of Bolivia's debt. This represents a remarkable change in Japan's traditional approach to debt forgiveness. It is much to be hoped that the British and German governments will soon follow Japan's lead.

Like most indebted poor countries Bolivia has been forced to adopt a structural adjustment programme as the condition for the rescheduling of its international debt. Structural adjustment programmes are packages of economic adjustments and budgetary constraints imposed on each indebted poor country by the International Monetary Fund and the World Bank (and in Bolivia's case the Inter-American Development Bank as well) as the condition for the rescheduling of external debt to creditor governments and private banking. Rescheduling means that structural adjustment loans are extended to indebted poor countries in the form of interest payments to external debtors. New money does not reach the indebted poor country, though it is added to their external debt. The purpose of structural adjustment loans is to prevent the indebted country from defaulting on its debt, and thus to protect the interests of the commercial banks, governments and international financial institutions who hold the debt. While governments and bankers in the North are rewarded for their poor lending decisions the people of indebted poor countries are subjected to economic 'austerity' as a means of redirecting national wealth towards maximum debt repayment.

In Bolivia's case, as in the case of all indebted poor countries subjected to structural adjustment, austerity is a euphemism for extreme poverty, hunger and death. In 1986, when Bolivia was diverting more than half its export earnings to debt repayments, 47 per cent of Bolivia's children and 50 per cent of rural women were malnourished, and four out of ten children died before their fifth birthday. In the 1990s, 20 per cent of Bolivians still do not live to reach the age of forty, 33 per cent have no access to health services or safe water, 40 per cent of children do not complete even five years of schooling, 70 per cent of Bolivians live in extreme poverty and the child mortality rate is the highest in Latin America.

Various generals ruled Bolivia for decades and it was these military dictators who stole the country's wealth, past and future, borrowing 80 per cent of its external debt. Besides paying for military hardware, government loans were supposed to have been used to build roads, and an oil refinery which, at $200 million, was possibly the most expensive refinery in the world, and one which has never operated at more than 30 per cent capacity (George, 1988). Much of the debt was stolen by the generals for their own private use. In 1982, having bled the country dry, the generals handed Bolivia back to civilian government. The newly elected civilian government at first refused the International Monetary Fund's austerity package and was consequently cut off from any new loans or foreign investment. In 1986 Bolivia adopted a structural adjustment programme and is regarded as a success story of adjustment by the International Monetary Fund and the World Bank. Along with Uganda, it has been so compliant with the adjustment regimen that it is now eligible for some very limited debt remission under the current highly indebted poor country debt relief scheme (see Chapter 4).

But a success story for Bolivia's bankers has been a disaster for Bolivia's people. Under the strictures of structural adjustment client states of the International Monetary Fund and World Bank are required to reduce public spending. This typically means reducing spending on education, housing and medical care, and abandoning efforts to provide clean piped water and sewers. The other measures imposed under structural adjustment programmes include: reorienting the economy towards export production of primary (mostly agricultural) commodities; freezing or reducing wages; devaluing the currency (to lower the value of exports and hence increase their volume and 'competitiveness'); removing subsidies on the prices of basic foodstuffs; privatizing state enterprises; deregulating banking and trade, removing all tariffs and protection for local banks, industry and farmers; removing restrictions or regulations on foreign investment; and reducing labour and environmental protection.

In Bolivia's case these structural adjustment requirements saw spending on education fall by 40 per cent from 1980 to 1993, on health by 30 per cent and on housing by 77 per cent. Bolivia also suffered from big falls in the price of all its primary commodity exports, including tin, natural gas and soya beans. Such falls were an indirect, though not unforeseeable, consequence of the global impact of structural adjustment.

Under structural adjustment the International Monetary Fund and the World Bank forced more than eighty indebted poor countries in the 1980s to increase the volume of their primary commodity exports, resulting in major declines in primary commodity prices. Many observers in both North and South regard this consequence of global structural adjustment as deliberate. The consequence was that North America, Japan and Europe were able to buy primary commodities such as timber, ores and minerals, and agricultural products such as animal feed, fruits, cereals, coffee and tea, at prices substantially lower in the 1990s than they had been paying in the 1970s. As the Latin American economist Xabier Gorostiaga puts it, the International Monetary Fund and the World Bank through structural adjustment generated a transfer of resources from poor to rich countries in the 1980s and 1990s 'comparable to the worst pillage of colonial days' (Gorostiaga, 1993).

The avowed intention of structural adjustment is to stimulate growth, to increase the amount of money available for debt repayment, and so eventually to reduce the amount of debt owing. However, even according to these narrowly economic criteria, structural adjustment has failed. In exchange for allowing Western bankers to guide their economies according to the latest principles of deregulated free market economics, most indebted poor countries saw big increases in unemployment, declines in Gross Domestic Product, declining levels of private investment, reductions in the total value of exports (though large increases in volume), and stagnation in the level of manufacturing output. Even the level of debt continues to rise in most indebted poor countries under structural adjustment. The World Bank projects that, provided Bolivia sticks to its structural adjustment conditions, Bolivia's external debt will continue to rise until 2001 before beginning to decline in the first and second decades of the next millennium.

There are a number of reasons why structural adjustment has had such deleterious effects on indebted country economies. First, structural adjustment forced all indebted poor countries to abandon import substitution, which had become a key post-colonial strategy for economic growth in developing countries. This was the central economic strategy of the East Asian 'tiger economies' such as Korea and Singapore, where a mix of government and private investment was directed towards the establishment of agricultural and manufacturing capacity in key imports such as rice, cooking oil, steel and concrete, clothes and textiles, shoes, televisions, telephones, and more recently cars and computers. Significant tariffs were imposed on imported goods to establish a favourable market for local products (Mommen, 1996). Import substitution favours local production for local consumption and enables countries to achieve self-sufficiency in the key economic activities of agriculture, textiles and construction without which a country cannot feed, clothe and house its own people. Import substitution also enables a country to achieve a diverse export production capacity instead of being dependent for its export earnings on one or two primary commodities such as tin or coffee (Bello, 1996).

It was precisely this strategy of pursuing self-sufficiency through import substitution and tariff barriers which in the nineteenth and early twentieth centuries was pursued by many governments in Europe and North America. The European Union, Japan and the United States continue to use agricultural subsidies, market interventions and tariffs to achieve food self-sufficiency and to generate food surpluses, and to protect core industries including textiles, construction, electrical goods and car manufacture. By disallowing tariff protection for local agricultural production and for nascent local industries in the South, and by discouraging public and private investment in productive capacity, structural adjustment drives many state and private industries into liquidation. It also reduces the capacity of adjusted nations to provide affordable food, clothes and housing for their own poorest peoples.

A second reason for the deleterious effects of structural adjustment is that no discrimination is made between spending for public investment and public expenditure for other purposes. By drastically cutting spending on social budgets, structural adjustment reduces the education and skill level of the workforce, as the Bolivian case illustrates particularly sharply. Adjustment also undermines the public infrastructure on which agricultural and industrial development depend, thus contributing to a downward economic spiral. By contrast, in the East Asian economies substantial public funds were directed to education and training, and also to those basic forms of infrastructural investment necessary for industrial development including water and drainage, electricity, transportation and telecommunication networks.

A third reason why structural adjustment fails to achieve its stated objective of advancing economic development is that it generates increased internal inequality within indebted poor countries. A key factor in the economic achievements of the East Asian economies was land reform. Taiwan, Korea and Japan all inaugurated land reform programmes after the Second World War. By putting more resources in the hands of poor people these programmes helped to reduce inequality and so to pave the way for subsequent advances in development. Inequality is a major threat to economic uplift because it lowers the capacity of the poor to participate in social life and in economic markets. In the end even the rich and comfortable lose out in very unequal societies because such societies are characterized by increased social stress, crime, ill health and public disorder.

The Philippine economist Walden Bello argues that while structural adjustment failed to promote economic growth in indebted countries, it was highly successful in opening up these poor countries to imports from rich northern countries, and in providing rich pickings of cheap primary commodities such as tropical hardwoods, soy beans, maize, coffee, tin and bauxite.

Bello believes that these achievements were part of an under-lying global economic strategy from the North, to increase the dependence of post-colonial economies on the northern powers and their multinational corporations.

Bello's post-colonial critique of structural adjustment, and his suspicion that it is a part of a larger global strategy on the part of the rich North to keep the South in poverty and dependence while sustaining profits in the North, is widely shared among non-governmental organizations and economists in the South (Bello, 1996). V. Anantha-Nagaswaren, another economist from the South, who works for Crédit Suisse bank in Switzerland, expresses this view very succinctly:

> Western lenders lend recklessly in good times and when the loans fail, they are bailed out, stringent and contractory conditions are imposed on the borrowing governments, asset prices collapse and a vast majority of the population is made poorer. Foreign investors then walk into markets prised open for them by the IMF and pick up assets cheaply. This modern bloodless colonialism is very neat. (Jubilee 2000, 1998)

Like Bello, the Egyptian economist Samir Amin argues that far from structural adjustment having 'failed' it has in fact been highly successful in terms of the economic interests of its sponsors, the governments of the North and the corporate and banking sectors of northern economies. Just as the excess amount of debt built up in the South in the 1970s and early 1980s was a highly effective means of deploying idle capital in the international banking system, so the subsequent structural adjustment of poor economies in the South, and in Eastern Europe, continues to allow the 'free mobility of capital to prevail' over humanitarian or developmental considerations (Amin, 1997). High interest rates are part of the same logic. They enable floating capital to achieve a high return, even though it is not productively invested, while at the same time they enable the United States to maintain its own enormous external debt, and hence military prowess, by capital inflows from the South, and 'forced borrowings from its partners' (Amin, 1997).

Amin argues that the excessive levels of debt and the regressive development which debt and adjustment have brought about in the South are not unintended consequences of international capital management. Rather they are means for managing the current phase of global capitalism in which the dynamics of the global economy are increasingly moving outside the political and social control of nation states, and in which the amount of money in circulation exceeds by a factor of fifty the amount of goods and services which are produced. In this context, structural adjustment is a global mechanism imposed by strong nations on weak ones for maximizing returns on the large and expanding pool of speculative capital, which is mostly controlled in the North. Enforced devaluations have the effect of undervaluing poor country labour, productive plant and natural resources. Combined with floating exchange rates, devaluations provide significant opportunities for speculative capital profit-taking.

Similarly, privatization of essential services such as water, energy and transport provides a risk-free means for mopping up excess capital without that capital being invested in new enterprises and reducing unemployment. And whereas governments often use the public monopoly of service provision to correct inequalities and meet human development objectives, private capital uses the same monopoly purely to enhance profits: 'returns obtained by capital under these conditions aggravate inequality in the state's subsequent capacity to intervene so as to palliate the negative effects of globalization' (Amin, 1997).

Increased unemployment in the North and the South is also a direct consequence of adjustment. Again this is not unintended, but part of the logic of adjusting weak nations and poor communities to the increased profitability of the capital base of strong nations and corporations. As Amin says:

> The rise of unemployment over the past twenty-five years has been produced not by the market, but by the strategies

of capital. Unemployment is desired by the capitalist state as a necessary means to destroy the achievements of the workers' movement. This proposition applies both to the developed capitalist West and to the reconquered countries of the East. There is no reason to believe the speeches of those in power as they lament unemployment. In the peripheries of the capitalist system, poverty and unequal distribution of income are not negative effects produced by specific circumstances or mistaken policies. They are the product of the system's logic, the logic of world polarization immanent in the system itself. (Amin, 1997)

The internationalization and deregulation of banking helps in this global adjustment project, allowing for savings from the South (and the East) to be transformed into speculative capital profits in the North (Amin, 1997).

Further evidence for Amin's argument that structural adjustment is not failing but succeeding in its underlying objectives relates to the variable application of adjustment as between rich and poor countries. Thus while indebted poor countries are required to devalue their currencies, create unemployment and close schools and hospitals in order to adjust their economies to debt servicing, rich countries like the USA with its very large public debt maintain public spending on social programmes, subsidies to farmers, infrastructural improvements and military hardware.

Amin's analysis highlights the fact that the economic web in which indebted poor countries are caught up is not the consequence of blind or ineluctable global market forces. On the contrary it is the creation of those countries in the North which have the strongest economies and the greatest wealth and political prowess, and of the economic institutions, such as the International Monetary Fund, which they control. The IMF is seen by many as an international body whose economic policies are designed primarily to serve the foreign policy interests of the United States of America, the host of the IMF and its biggest contributor (Feldstein, 1998). The pursuit by the IMF of free trade and financial, labour and environmental deregulation is part of a much larger Western economic project whose ultimate end is to direct the national economies of the world into a new 'utopia' of an integrated liberalized global market of capital, labour and goods (Gray, 1998). Although the stated outcome of this putatively 'utopian' project is improvements in material standards for all, in reality extreme economic liberalization of this kind is enhancing the power and profits of capital and corporations relative to the rights and earnings of workers, and the earnings of rich nations relative to poor ones.

The last time the world system embraced financial deregulation and economic liberalization on this scale was in the latter part of the nineteenth century and the early part of the twentieth. Fascism flourished among the millions whom that experiment impoverished, and especially in the Great Depression of the 1920s and 1930s. This last great global experiment in free trade and economic liberalism fomented a whole series of global conflicts culminating in 1939 in the Second World War. The current liberalization project has similarly spawned a whole host of new ethnic and religious conflicts which, through migration and international terrorism, even threaten its sponsoring nations in the North.

Development economists now refer to the 1980s, when adjustment was in its early phases, as the lost decade. The indices of human welfare declined in most developing countries because of the social conditions imposed by the debt burden and structural adjustment. According to the World Bank itself the number of people living in absolute poverty grew in the 1980s from 130 to 190 million in Latin America alone. Structural adjustment was supposed to shift emphasis and resources from urban to rural economies, and from middle-class to poorer people. But, as the President of the Inter-American Development Bank, Enrique Iglesias, reports, 'the bulk of the costs of adjustment fell disproportionately on the middle and low-income groups, while the top five per cent of the population retained or, in some cases, even increased its standard of living' (Iglesias, 1992). The number of absolutely poor in Africa, which has the greatest concentration of indebted poor countries undergoing IMF enforced structural adjustment, has consequently risen to 200 million of the region's 690 million people, and the World Bank projects this will rise to 300 million by the year 2000. Furthermore, Africa's income per head has fallen to levels equivalent to those obtaining at the time of independence in the early 1960s.

Millions have suffered, and many have died, from malnutrition and from preventable diseases such as tuberculosis, cholera and diarrhoea since the imposition of structural adjustment. Millions more have had their life prospects blighted by lack of education, unemployment and environmental degradation. In addition many indebted poor countries have experienced a collapse of public order as crime and violence have become endemic. The growth and manufacture of narcotics (cocaine in Bolivia) has also risen sharply. Even as the US government seeks military solutions to drug production in extremely indebted countries such as Bolivia and Peru, US bankers continue to impose structural adjustment programmes which drive smallholders into the production of the only primary commodity, the opium poppy, whose price has not collapsed on world markets. The quantity of drugs on the streets of the US is part of what Susan George calls the 'debt boomerang'. So too is the pressure of immigration from impoverished African, Asian and Latin American nations at the borders of the USA and the European Union (George, 1992).

Non-governmental organizations, churches, labour unions and other citizens' groups in the South and the North have consistently highlighted the tragic effects of structural adjustment on the peoples of indebted nations. They have also pointed to its negative impacts on small enterprises and farms, and on the efforts of indebted countries to achieve food security, to protect their environments, and to enhance domestic productive capacity. Through a variety of vehicles they have challenged the Bank to incorporate local populations, their organizations and their knowledge into the definition and design of national economic programmes and in other ways to democratize the economic policy-making process.

In 1997, after years of resisting pressure to change, the World Bank set up what it calls a structural adjustment participatory review initiative, which was born through a dialogue between the new World Bank President, James Wolfensohn, and critics of the Bank. The review is being implemented in eight countries by national coalitions that are bringing together non-governmental organizations, churches, labour unions, farmers' associations, women's groups and chambers of commerce.

The structural adjustment participatory review initiative is a sign that the World Bank, though not the International Monetary Fund, is at last beginning to admit the need for radical reforms to adjustment programmes. But for such moral reforms of a macroeconomic project to be enacted, the goals of the project, and of its sponsoring organizations, would have to be radically altered. There is little evidence from the annual meetings and reports of the World Bank and IMF that such a reorientation is envisaged. On the contrary the International Monetary Fund in 1998 sought a fundamental change in its own constitutive articles which would make the enforcement and advancement of global financial and trade deregulation a central goal of its future operations. This change would also tie future economic rescue packages to financial and trade deregulation on the part of beneficiary nation states (Feldstein, 1998).

David Budhoo, an official of the International Monetary Fund, expressed his deep sense of moral guilt at his own role in enforcing adjustment on impoverished nations in the following words:

> Today I resigned from the staff of the International Monetary Fund after over twelve years, and 1,000 days of official Fund work in the field, hawking your medicines and your bag of tricks to governments and to people in Latin America and the Caribbean and Africa. To me resignation is a priceless liberation, for with it I have taken the first big step to that place where I may hope to wash my hands of what in my mind's eye is the blood of millions of poor and starving peoples ... the blood is so much, it runs in rivers. It dries up too; it cakes all over me.

Sometimes I feel there is not enough soap in the whole
world to cleanse me from the things that I did in your
name. (David Budhoo in Joseph, 1991)

The need for reform in the operations of the Bank and the
International Monetary Fund, and in particular the abandonment of structural adjustment, is urgent. Equally important are
reforms to the international financial system which will permit
a fairer distribution of the earth's limited resources than that
which has obtained under both colonial and post-colonial
economic arrangements. It is the maintenance of this historic
system of resource transfer from South to North that the
operations and policies of the World Bank and the International
Monetary Fund are currently still designed to service.

Structural Sin and the People of God

The failure of economists and bankers to recognize or respond
to the humanitarian and moral consequences of structural
adjustment is a classic instance of the reality of sin. The biblical
story of the origin of evil in human affairs, the myth of Adam
and Eve hiding from God in the Garden of Eden, confirms what
we learn from childhood: that sin is the denial of relationship,
the refusal of open, honest face-to-face engagement with God
and with persons whom we sin against. In the case of structural
adjustment this refusal is not just a personal refusal. It is a
refusal to confess openly that there is a connection between
high standards of living and rising affluence in the developed
world and the oppression and death which the poor experience
in Bolivia and Peru, Mozambique and Malawi, even though
this connection is clearly implied in the goals and procedures of
global economic management.

The father of liberation theology, the Peruvian theologian
Gustavo Gutiérrez, called this connection, and the refusal to
acknowledge it, 'structural sin'. The liberation theologians of
Latin America emphasize that sin has a social as well as a
personal dimension, and that the structures of economy,
politics and society may be described as sinful, as well as the
actions of individuals within these structures. Drawing on the

dependency theory of Fernando Henrique Cardoso, Gutiérrez argues that the poor of Latin America are ensnared in international economic structures which generate economic dependency among former colonized peoples, to make their raw materials and their labour available for continued low cost exploitation by the former colonizers: 'Development must attack the root causes of the problems and among them the deepest is economic, social, political, and cultural dependence of some countries upon others – an expression of the domination of some social classes over others' (Gutiérrez, 1988).

The advocates of dependency theory are often criticized for being too simplistic, blaming the conditions within developing countries entirely on external factors such as world markets, multinational corporations or international financial institutions such as the World Bank and the International Monetary Fund. Western economists who support structural adjustment argue that the poor remain poor in many developing countries because of internal corruption, the absence of the rule of law, and the abuse of political authority by dictators and corrupt governments. Structural adjustment is said to be designed to correct these problems by refocusing economic activity on private individuals rather than on government spending, which often fails because of corruption.

However, Gutiérrez points out in the first edition of his *Theology of Liberation* that internal political corruption is often sustained by external economic partners and their infusions of funds into corrupt regimes (Gutiérrez, 1971). This linkage between external influence and funds with internal corruption and the demise of the rule of law would seem to be newly validated by the consequences of structural adjustment in Bolivia, Peru and much of the rest of Latin America in the 1980s. While there was a move toward more democratic government in Latin America in the 1980s, whose roots preceded structural adjustment in most cases, popular support for fledgling democratic structures is being undermined by the World Bank and International Monetary Fund's imposition of economic stringencies which increase absolute poverty.

Austerity programmes have also had the effect of enhancing

the anti-democratic power of the small number of families, favoured by colonial and post-colonial regimes, who still own so much of the land in Latin America. By refocusing economic effort upon agricultural exports, adjustment has had the effect of increasing the feudal power of large landowners in post-colonial Latin American societies. Numerous civil and terrorist conflicts over land in Latin America witness to this problem, such as the violent struggle of the Shining Path guerrillas in Peru, the struggles over land in the Amazon, and the continuing uprising of peasant and Indian farmers in Chiapas, Mexico which has been so brutally suppressed by the Mexican military and government-supported paramilitary groups.

In response to criticism of dependency theory, Gutiérrez argues in a new edition of his *Theology of Liberation* that dependency theorists have heaped too much blame on external actors, and ignored the degree to which internal political and economic imbalances were the product of internal cultural, moral and social conditions, albeit exacerbated by external forces:

> It is clear ... that the theory of dependence, which was so extensively used in the early years of our encounter with the Latin American world, is now an inadequate tool, because it does not take sufficient account of the internal dynamics of each country or of the vast dimensions of the world of the poor. (Gutiérrez, 1988)

Similarly, Gutiérrez now emphasizes the personal consent to sin which underlies sinful structures. For sinful structures to be built and sustained requires the actions and consent of sinful people. As Gutiérrez puts it, 'behind an unjust structure there is a personal or collective will responsible – a willingness to reject God and neighbour' (Gutiérrez, 1990). And just as the rejection of God and neighbour is centrally implicated in the corruption and injustice sustained by contemporary economic and political structures, both within Latin America and beyond, so the appropriate response, according to Gutiérrez, is not a political revolution, nor even the total overthrow of the capitalist system, but rather spiritual and moral renewal.

In this respect Gutiérrez highlights two central features of the reform and renewal programme of liberation theology. The first is that the poor have the gospel preached to them. The 'preferential option for the poor' is a central feature of liberation theology. It involves the belief that God looks with special favour on the poor and that the poor are closer to the kingdom of God than the rich. This belief has biblical roots in the story of the Exodus when Yahweh rescues the Hebrews from slavery, and in the teaching of Jesus who so frequently identified the poor, debtors and outcasts as the inheritors of the Kingdom, and warned the rich and powerful of impending judgement. It also has unequivocal backing from Pope John Paul II, though he has resisted other elements of the liberation theology programme. In his encyclical letter *Libertatis Conscientia* he acknowledges that the mission to and of the poor involves both meeting their immediate needs and promoting 'structural changes in society so as to secure conditions of life worthy of the human person' (John Paul II, 1989).

The option for the poor has entailed sharp criticism of the former alliance between the Catholic Church and the ruling oligarchies of Latin America in the post-colonial era. This alliance sacralized the corrupt economics and undemocratic politics which characterized the whole region until the 1980s, and are still widespread. The systematic denial of human rights, the misappropriation of government loans and tax revenues for military programmes, or for personal gain, the theft of land from peasants and native peoples, all were quietly ignored – some would say condoned – by the church hierarchy before the advent of the liberation theology movement.

The second feature of the reform and renewal programme of liberation theology that Gutiérrez particularly highlights is the fostering of *communidades ecclesiale de base*, communities of the poor who witness to the reality of evangelical love and Christian hope. In these communities the poor are not only addressed by the message of the Kingdom, they are also Kingdom bearers and are reforming and renewing the Church as Church from below instead of Church from above (Gutiérrez, 1990).

The Catholic Church has traditionally identified the being or *esse* of the church with the hierarchy of Pope, cardinals and clerics. But at the Second Vatican Council in the 1960s a new recognition was given to the idea that the people of God are themselves the true embodiment of the sacramental presence of Christ on earth. This partial laicization of the doctrine of the Church not only catalysed internal ecclesial reforms (some of which the present Pope has reversed), but also foreshadowed the emergence of democracy in many Catholic countries in the decades following the Council (Huntington, 1993).

The Latin American *communidades ecclesiale de base* were some of the first exemplars of this ecclesiastical reform movement. Members of these base communities studied the Bible for themselves. From their reading of the Bible they critiqued the social structures and conditions which were keeping them poor while at the same time recognizing the Messianic status of their poverty. In other words in these base communities people began to discover that their own experience of poverty was also an opportunity. Their poverty brought them closer to an identity with Jesus Christ who 'makes himself present precisely through those who are "absent" from the banquet (see Luke 14.15–24), those who are not the great ones of the world, the respected, "the wise and understanding" (Matthew 11.25)' (Gutiérrez, 1990).

But this identity with Christ is not an opiate, an occasion for quelling the desire for justice or the pursuit of social change. On the contrary, the evangelical commitment and Messianic fervour of the base communities enabled them to organize themselves and their neighbours more effectively in self-help and community-building projects, and in challenging the injustices visited upon them by landowners, city authorities, factory owners and corrupt politicians:

The problems most often addressed (by base communities) turn toward the communities' need for clean water, sewage disposal, electricity, paved roads, food and education for children, health care, and job skills. In areas where land reform is a key issue, the process of conscientization and organizing can lead to strongly conflictual situations. At some point efforts at 'self-help' run into unjust structures that block the possibility of further development ... Most work of base communities, however, involves cooperative efforts of members rather than struggles of conflict, and the groups clearly opt for non-violent methods of change. (McGovern, 1989)

According to Gutiérrez, the central task of the base communities of the poor in reforming the Church is to name the absence of God from the Church which is demonstrated when the Church ignores the unjust conditions which oppress the poor. For the history of salvation and the history of human society are not two different histories but one (Gutiérrez, 1977). The Church is the sacrament of salvation within human history and the people of God who are the Church remain the people of the covenant which God first made with the people of Israel. As John Paul II puts it:

The situation of the poor is a situation contrary to the covenant. This is why the law of the covenant protects them by means of precepts that reflect the attitude of God when God liberated Israel from the slavery of Egypt. Injustice to the little ones and the poor is a grave sin, which destroys communion with God. (John Paul II, 1989)

The reform of the Catholic Church in Latin America which the liberation theology movement has helped achieve has presaged the emergence of new religious, political and ethnic pluralisms in Latin America. Protestant and Pentecostal churches are now flourishing. Many of them are located in very poor communities and, like the base communities, these new religious groups are enabling the poor to find a voice and to find personal and moral resources in the struggle to improve their economic situation (Martin, 1996).

Many indigenous groups, including Mayans in Central America, and Indians in Bolivia and other parts of the Andes region, are finding in these religious developments a new religio-cultural identity. This new identity seems to provide a stronger ground for hope than the paternalism of the Catholic Church, and empowers poor and indigenous peoples in their demands for an end to internal racism and for land reform after hundreds of years of colonial and post-colonial oppression and land theft.

The internal reform and democratization of the Catholic Church also preceded, and to a certain extent catalysed, the emergence both of democratic government, and of a strengthened civil society, in many Latin American countries in the 1980s (Huntington, 1991). Together these processes of pluralization constitute the emergence or strengthening of both democratic process and civil society in the region (Gorostiaga, 1993). But, as we have seen, there is a real danger that the extreme austerity measures which are still being forced on emergent democratic governments by the International Monetary Fund, in partnership with the World Bank and northern creditor governments, will undermine the legitimacy of democracy, unravel the bonds of civil society, and subvert the rule of law in the region, all of which will hinder and not help the possibility of genuine political reform and economic uplift.

Whatever the limitations of earlier dependency theory, it is evident that structural adjustment has introduced a new and deeply damaging kind of subservient dependency of indebted poor governments on northern bankers with their economic straitjackets. A dependency which drives peoples from the land into unemployment and hunger, which creates ecological collapse, and which fosters civil war, terrorism, drug dealing and criminality on a massive scale, is clearly a denial of God, who is revealed in the Bible as having a particular care for the poor, and whose laws require a fair sharing of the earth's resources.

Sources

Samir Amin (1997), *Capitalism in the Age of Globalization* (London: Zed Books)

Walden Bello (1996), 'Structural Adjustment Programs: "Success" for Whom?' in Jerry Mander and Edward Goldsmith (eds.), *The Case against the Global Economy and for a Turn toward the Local* (San Francisco: Sierra Club Books)

Martin Feldstein (1998), 'Refocusing the IMF', *Foreign Affairs* (March) volume 77

John Garrett, Joseph Hanlon and Ann Pettifor (1998), *In Our Own Back Yard: Britain and the Debt Crisis: Time is Running Out* (London, Jubilee 2000 Coalition)

Susan George (1992), *The Debt Boomerang: How Third World Debt Harms Us All* (London, Pluto Press)

Xabier Gorostiaga (1993), 'Latin America in the New World Order' in Jeremy Brecher, John Brown Childs and Jill Cutler, *Global Visions: Beyond the New World Order* (Boston, MA: South End Press)

John Gray (1998), *False Dawn: The Delusions of Global Capitalism* (London: Granta Books)

Gustavo Gutiérrez (1971), *A Theology of Liberation* (Eng. trans., London: SCM Press)

Gustavo Gutiérrez (1988), *A Theology of Liberation* (Eng. trans., revised edition, London: SCM Press)

Gustavo Gutiérrez (1990), *The Truth Shall Make You Free: Confrontations* (Eng. trans., Maryknoll, NY: Orbis Books)

Samuel Huntington (1991), *The Third Wave: Democratization in the Late Twentieth Century* (Norman, OKL: University of Oklahoma Press)

Enrique Iglesias (1992), *Reflections on Economic Development: Toward a New Latin American Consensus* (Washington, DC: Inter-American Development Bank)

John Paul II (1989), *Libertatis Conscientia* (London: Catholic Truth Society)

M. P. Joseph (1991), 'A Third World Viewpoint' in *Third World Debt – First World Responsibility* (Edinburgh: Centre for Theology and Public Issues)

Arthur F. McGovern (1989), *Liberation Theology and Its Critics: Toward an Assessment* (Maryknoll, NY: Orbis Books)

David Martin (1996), *Forbidden Revolutions* (London: SPCK)

André Mommen (1996), 'The Asian Miracle: A Critical Reassessment' in Alex E. Fernández Jilberto and André Mommen (eds.), *Liberalization in the Developing World: Institutional and Economic Changes in Latin America, Africa and Asia* (London: Routledge)

Organizations

The addresses and websites of organizations (and some of their representatives) with primary responsibility for structural adjustment programmes are listed below. Letters, e-mails and faxes to these organizations from concerned citizens of their funding countries play an important part in challenging their undemocratic and secretive control of more than eighty economies in the South.

Michel Camdessus *Managing Director*, International Monetary Fund, 700 19th Street N.W., Washington, D.C. 20431, USA
Tel: (202) 623–7000 *Fax:* (202) 623-4661

Evangelos A. Calamitsis *African Department Director*, International Monetary Fund, 700 19th Street N.W., Washington, D.C. 20431, USA

Hubert Neiss *Asia and Pacific Department Director*, International Monetary Fund, 700 19th Street N.W., Washington, D.C. 20431, USA

Christian Brachet *Director*, Office in Europe, International Monetary Fund, 64–66, Avenue d'Iena, 75116 Paris, France
Tel: (33–1) 40 69 30 70 *Fax:* (33–1) 47 23 40 89

Alan A. Tait *Director*, Office in Geneva, International Monetary Fund, 58, Rue de Moillebeau, 1209 Geneva, Switzerland
Tel: (41–22) 918 03 00 *Fax:* (41–22) 918 03 03
http://www.imf.org/

James D. Wolfensohn *President*, The World Bank, 1818 H St., NW, Washington, D.C. 20433, USA
E-mail: devforum@worldbank.org
http://www.worldbank.org/html/extdr/backgrd/ibrd/role.htm

The IMF and the World Bank receive most of their funding from the G7 countries which are comprised of Canada, France, Germany, Japan, the Netherlands, UK and USA. Letters to government ministers in these countries calling for an end to the poverty, suffering and death caused by the imposition of structural adjustment programmes as condition for debt repayment play an important part in alerting the partners and funders of these institutions to citizen concern. The governors of the International Monetary Fund include the following government representatives:

US Secretary of the Treasury Robert Rubin *Department of Treasury*, 1500 Pennsylvania Avenue NW, Washington DC 20220, USA
E-mail: dale.servetnick@treas.sprint.com

Hikaru Matsunaga, *Minister of Finance*, 1–1 Kasumigaseki 3-chome, Chiyoda-ku, Tokyo, Japan

Federal Minister of Finance Postfach 1308, D-53003 Bonn, Germany

Gordon Brown *Chancellor of the Exchequer*, HM Treasury, Parliament Street, London SW1P 3AG
E-mail: info@hm-treasury.gov.uk

3 Global Trade and the Deepening of World Poverty

Growing Bananas in Costa Rica for British Supermarkets

My name is Eldora Fuentes and I started working on the estate when I was thirteen. I met my husband here and we have five children. It is a bad place to bring up the children but we have no choice as we are too poor to move elsewhere. The worst thing is the pesticides. The whole place smells of them, even our tiny house, and the chemicals run into the streams and drainage ditches round the house where the children play. Even the water from the well we use smells of chemicals and I am sure it is contaminated but the company say they have tested it and it is safe to drink.

My job right now involves spraying the individual banana plants with a backpack sprayer. I am off sick because my toenails are affected by the Gramoxone which we spray. They have been peeling off and the new ones are coming through black. My workmates have similar problems. We don't get protective clothing, not even masks or gloves, although we ask for them. We never received any kind of training on how to use these chemicals. And even though we wear boots, your feet still get wet, because the chemicals run down your legs.

My husband's job is mainly in harvesting. He has to remove the plastic bags which have pesticide in them from the fruits which are ready for harvesting, and then cut the heavy branches and hook them on to the overhead wires where they are pulled along to the packing plant. He too gets sick from the pesticides.

They also spray the plants from the plane which flies overhead and everyone, all the workers, gets sprayed. Nobody is protected. The plane flies over the houses too, although they switch off the spray, but some always escapes and the pesticide mist is carried by the breeze. My children have been affected. If you go outside when they are spraying you get white marks on your skin. Many people get ill but the doctors round here are all in the hands of the companies. We work from six in the morning till six at night. We don't get proper breaks for lunch or anything and when I come back I feel dizzy and weak from working all day with toxic chemicals, and sometimes I vomit.

There is an *asociacione solidarista* (solidarity union) here. The company started it as a sop for unionists who wanted representation and everyone has to join it. But it does nothing to help us. The company will do anything to stop proper unions. My parents were unionists, and when I was pregnant the first time, the boss made me go out into the fields to collect canes, even when I was six months pregnant, and another time he sent me to spread fertilizer on the fields. I was worried that my baby would be affected by the fertilizer.

The wages are very low and they have been cutting salaries. My pay was cut from 45,000 *colones* a week to 12,000 *colones* a week (£31). This is because I was seen talking to a unionist and when I began to talk about workers' rights with my workmates, the management heard about it. The boss told me, 'You must do what I tell you to do. I can pay you whatever I feel like and anyone who doesn't like this can leave. If it doesn't suit you here, there are plenty more banana workers out there.' It is so easy for the management to sack us because they hire us from subcontractors for three months at a time.

They won't allow unionists on to the plantation. If you complain they try to sack you or spread rumours about you. They say, 'Don't speak to her, she is a unionist.' It is really hard. Our own workmates who were once our friends won't speak to us any more. They are scared of the management. The companies will do anything to stop unionists. The son of a unionist was nearly killed last year on the next estate to this one. He was sent into a big tank used for mixing up pesticide to clean it with a bucket-load of acid. These tanks are normally cleaned with hoses, and they are dangerous – no one ever goes inside. The boy collapsed after a few minutes in the tank. When they found him he was nearly dead. All his skin peeled off, on his shoulders, his arms, legs and stomach. It was terrible and it looks like they wanted to kill him because his father had almost succeeded in starting a union.

It is very hard looking after the children here as well. I worry about them getting ill from the chemicals. The house is provided by the company but it is little more than one room and the money we get is not enough. It is expensive to send the children to school. They need 5,000 *colones* every month for books and lunch and we just can't manage for all the children, but if they don't go to school they won't have any hope of getting away from here, or going to college so they can get a proper job.

I get very depressed. I am thirty-nine and I have been working on this plantation my whole life. Sometimes you can just see the mountains from the higher slopes of the plantation and it looks so lovely. But it is so ugly here. Just squat banana trees and mud and then all the fruits on the trees are covered in those plastic bags with pesticide inside. Costa Rica is a beautiful country, a peaceful country, it even has no army. Most people not on the estates get good education and health care but we seem to be left out, even though the bananas we grow help to make the country richer.

The Expansion of Global Trade and the Growth of World Poverty

Bananas are the most widely eaten fruit in Britain and North America, and they are the second most valuable internationally traded fruit crop, after grapes. Most bananas sold in the UK used to come from former colonies under the Lomé Convention which protected Caribbean producers. These producers are mostly small farmers and they have better conditions of labour and use fewer chemicals than the US companies in Central America. But under pressure from multinationals and the World Trade Organization, the Lomé Convention is gradually being replaced by a European Union quota system which reduces protection for Caribbean producers. Consequently many UK supermarkets now sell bananas at exceptionally low prices bought from US companies whose plantations use armed guards to suppress union activity (Alexander and Donlan, 1997). They are sold at similarly low prices in the USA.

The Portuguese introduced bananas from Africa into their colonies in Central and South America in the eighteenth century. Bananas have played a key role in Costa Rica's economy since that time, but their production and marketing is still mostly controlled by foreign companies. One fifth of Costa Rica's export crop is controlled by Chiquita, and 60 per cent of global banana production is marketed by just three American companies, Chiquita, Del Monte and Dole. The economies of Costa Rica, Ecuador, Honduras and Panama are highly dependent on bananas which account for more than 20 per cent of their combined foreign exchange. However, the real price of bananas has been falling consistently on world markets for the last thirty years. Consequently these countries have given way to pressure from foreign banana companies to expand the estates and keep down production costs with anti-union measures and low environmental regulation. Costa Rica has doubled land under banana cultivation in the last ten years.

The expansion of banana production in Costa Rica was strongly opposed by local people and non-governmental agencies, including the churches in the Atlantic zone where cultivation is concentrated. Protests focused on the impact on human rights, the poor health and housing conditions on the plantations, and on environmental problems. Banana plantations are the main cause of deforestation in Costa Rica. They pollute rivers and coastlines with sediment which runs freely off deforested slopes, and with toxic chemicals at levels high enough to kill fish and animals as well as to harm human health. The most toxic pesticides are designed to attack the respiratory and nervous systems of pests. Research indicates that 45 per cent of plantation workers in Costa Rica experience intoxication effects from pesticides and fungicides. As well as harming the health of banana workers, these harmful chemicals have been found to persist in fruit at the point of sale.

The case of Costa Rican bananas is a microcosm of the effects of the expansion and deregulation of global trade in agricultural commodities, manufactured goods and finance which has occurred in the last twenty years. As we have seen, this expansion was partly fuelled by the structural adjustment regime imposed by the World Bank and the International Monetary Fund. Reductions in tariff barriers in industrial countries from 40 per cent in 1945 to an average 4 per cent today have played an even bigger role (Lockwood, 1997).

The last treaty of the Global Agreement on Tariffs and Trade (GATT), known as the Uruguay Round, imposed a new regime of tariff reductions and trade deregulation which disallowed agricultural subsidies to protect food production for local consumption in developing countries, and tariff barriers to protect their emerging industries (Jacobs, 1996). Under its rules child workers in Pakistan, Nepal and India may legitimately compete with workers in countries where child labour is outlawed (Goldsmith, 1996). Similarly it is illegal for countries to attempt to stem imports of goods whose production involves environmental destruction. The Uruguay Round also established a new international institution, the World Trade Organization – based in Geneva – which has a legislature, an executive and a judicial system with international powers to control global trade and to enforce this newly deregulated trade regimen.

Member nations accede by an act or statute in their own parliaments but subsequent democratic involvement is limited to biannual conferences of trade ministers from member countries. Most of the activities of the WTO are carried out by five hundred officials who operate without effective democratic and public scrutiny.

The primary aim of the World Trade Organization is to promote free trade and to adjudicate trading disputes between nations. However, its constitution does not enable it effectively to address the negative effects of the new global trading regime, such as the growing use of child labour and increasing environmental degradation. Nor do its articles permit it to work towards removing the protection which the Uruguay Round permitted to the economies of the North, and especially the USA and the European Union, even as it prescribed complete openness in the economies of the South. Like the International Monetary Fund, the WTO is said to be strongly influenced by US government opinion.

It is worth noting that the advisory committees of the WTO include many representatives of those multinational corporations which dominate trade in the principal internationally traded commodities, goods and services. Whether by design or accident, the new free-trade regime which the WTO advances and polices is enabling the world's largest companies – forty-seven of which control resources more valuable than the gross domestic product of most developing-country economies – to increase their control of global trade and pricing, at the expense of social and environmental conditions.

The combined effects of structural adjustment and the Uruguay Round are reorienting developing-country economies towards increased food production for export and reduced production for self-sufficiency and local consumption. This shift has involved the illegal and often violent eviction of vast numbers of small farmers and indigenous peoples from sustainable low-input subsistence farms and traditional nomadic areas to make land available for commercial cash-crop production. Much of this production is controlled by multinational corporations, five hundred of which control 70 per cent of global agricultural and manufacturing output. Conflicts over land are consequently igniting all over the developing world. For example, the ongoing Zapatista uprising in Chiapas, Mexico, which is being violently put down by the Mexican army and by paramilitaries funded by the Mexican government, is a consequence of the takeover of the lands of indigenous peoples by landowners and their private armies. Pressure to increase commercial agricultural output has grown because of the collapse of the Mexican currency and stock market in 1994. Attempts to resist land grabs and environmental destruction in other tropical regions including the Amazon region, Borneo and tropical central Africa have encountered similar private and state-supported violence.

Such mass evictions also have ecological as well as social costs. Millions are forced to move into the insanitary slums and shanty towns of cities which are growing into vast environmental disaster zones, their hinterlands often completely denuded of trees and shrubs as millions of rural–urban migrants search for fuel to cook or to keep warm. Millions of 'shifted cultivators' are forced to slash and burn in tropical forest or to cut fields out of steep hillsides in search of new land to feed themselves and their children (Northcott, 1996).

Deteriorating social and environmental conditions are evident in increasing poverty and destitution in many developing countries, and a massive rise in global inequality. The World Bank estimates that the number of absolutely poor in Latin America went up from 87 million in 1985 to 108 million in 1990. In sub-Saharan Africa, the most heavily indebted region, and the most reliant on agricultural commodity exports, there were 184 million living in absolute poverty in 1985 and 216 million in 1990 (Jacobs, 1996).

The World Bank takes the view that enforced migration (which, as we have seen, it has often funded with large loans) and the commercialization of agriculture are essential drivers to human development. Its economists view worsening social and ecological conditions as short-term problems which will ultimately be resolved by the economic growth generated by deregulated global trade (World Bank, 1992). But the Bank's own statistics seem to contradict this judgement. The Bank estimates that the Uruguay Round of the Global Agreement on Tariffs and Trade will increase the income of countries in the European Union by $80 billion to the year 2000 and of the United States and Japan by $50 billion. However, Latin America will see a net gain of only $5 billion while the continent of Africa will experience a net loss of $3 billion (Jacobs, 1996).

The new deregulated financial and trading system is also contributing to a growth in poverty and inequality in the 'rich' countries of the North as well as among the poor nations of the South, such that conditions of absolute poverty are now evident in many poor communities in the North. New Zealand and Britain privatized and deregulated their economies very rapidly in the 1980s and they have experienced the sharpest rise in internal inequality of any developed countries. In Britain today 1.5 million people live in housing categorized as unfit for human habitation. One quarter of all children live in households with less than half of average income, and hundreds of thousands are annually made homeless as a consequence of mortgage or rent arrears. Despite economic growth, unemployment remains high with 4 million either unemployed, registered unfit to work or in involuntary retirement. Many unemployed, such as those aged over fifty-five or under twenty-five, no longer even register in government statistics. Crime has increased tenfold compared with the 1950s and most of the increase has occurred in the last twenty years of economic deregulation and increased unemployment. Growing inequality has produced worsening health indices in poor communities, and has generated a sub-culture of exclusion from the mainstream of society, both of which tendencies have serious consequences for social cohesion (Jacobs, 1996; Northcott, 1998).

But Britain today has more millionaires than ever before and is exporting unprecedented amounts of capital to the global economy for investment in low-wage and low-regulation economies. Similarly in the South a small minority have benefited from the new global trading and finance regime with sharply increased wealth while millions are driven into poverty. There are hundreds of millionaires in Mexico today while poverty in Mexico has reached epidemic proportions.

The new global inequality is fomenting criminality and ethnic and civil conflict across the globe whose effects can be seen most vividly in countries such as Mexico, Colombia, Nigeria and Russia. The former Soviet Union experienced a massive drop in output of 50 per cent after the imposition of free market reforms and adjustments in 1989. Poverty levels rose to 37 per cent of the adult population in just three years between 1989 and 1992 and the death rate actually increased by 44 per cent. There is growing concern in the West at the international spread of criminal mafioso capitalism of the kind which has taken over much economic activity in the countries of the former Soviet Union as industrial and agricultural sectors have been 'freed' from state planning. The new poverty is also fuelling mass migration as we have seen. While sponsoring deregulated markets in natural resources and finance for the primary benefit of the corporations of the North, governments in the North resist the free movement of labour and are unwilling to receive the consequent waves of environmental and economic migrants.

Another key element in the globalization and disequalization of the world economy, as we have seen, is financial deregulation. Electronic computer networks have enhanced the expansionary effects of deregulation, and daily currency flows of up to a trillion dollars are now commonplace. The quantity of speculative capital flowing through the world's computerized dealing systems can have devastating effects on economies worldwide as the recent collapse in the supposedly successful 'emerging market' economies of East Asia and Latin America indicates.

The volume of international investment capital has also grown dramatically. In the new deregulated global economy companies are free to borrow money against increases in their share values, which have soared in the last twenty years, and to invest where the wages are lowest and the tax and regulatory regime the freest. Private investment is now judged by many development economists to be the key engine of economic growth and there is no doubt that it is more effective than the much smaller flows of international aid (and debt) at generating jobs. However, two thirds of this international investment still flows between the rich countries of the North. Of the $100 billion which went to developing countries in 1994, half went to the new industrialized countries of East Asia, one third to Latin America, 5 per cent to South Asia and only 3 per cent to Africa (Lockwood, 1997).

The new industrialized countries of East Asia experienced

extraordinary economic growth until the downturn in the region in 1997, partly as a consequence of this inward investment. They also experienced remarkable improvements in human welfare indices, in standards of living, and in levels of education. However, these economies do not conform to the deregulated market-led model of economic success purveyed around the indebted poor countries of Latin America and Africa, and the countries of the former Soviet bloc, by the World Bank and the International Monetary Fund. Taiwan, Korea and other countries in the region invested heavily in primary and secondary education, and directed significant state funds and loans towards infrastructural and industrial developments long before they became attractive locations for international capital. Malaysia strongly promoted education and skills training, while pursuing state-led economic plans, and sponsoring extensive publicly funded industrial investment. Singapore has also taken a very statist approach to wealth creation and wealth distribution, including a large state-controlled housing programme.

As the world has recently discovered, the economic advances of these new industrialized countries have not been won without cost. Nor are their financial and political structures beyond reproach, characterized as they have been by authoritarianism, economic corruption, suppression of internal dissent, government control of the media, and environmental abuse on a grand scale. Political and financial corruption combined with excessive external and internal debt, in addition to the actions of international currency speculators, brought about the economic collapse in the region in 1997. The environmental costs of rapid development have also been excessive. The whole region was shrouded in dangerous smog from vast forest fires in Java and Kalimantan in 1997, and temperatures have permanently risen to often intolerable levels in the urban areas of formerly lush tropical zones such as those of peninsular Malaysia and Thailand as well as Java, as the forest cover, and its cooling effects, have been traded for cash.

As the East Asian experience testifies, international investors, mostly based in Northern Europe, the United States, and

Japan, do not have vested interests in the advancement of democracy, the prevention of corruption or the maintenance of a decent environment in the foreign countries where they invest. The tragic explosion in 1984 of the Union Carbide battery factory, which had become surrounded by a squatter housing area in Bhopal in South India, killed hundreds of people, and permanently blighted the health of tens of thousands. Bhopal was just one example of the culpable human and environmental negligence commonly practised by multinational companies on poor communities, often with the complicity of corrupt local officials or government ministers.

While advocates of deregulated free markets argue that economic pluralism and open markets are precursors of political pluralism and democracy, there is a growing body of evidence that footloose international capital, operating outside the legal and ethical frameworks obtaining in the North, is often complicit in the maintenance of dictatorships through corrupt bribes, in the exploitation of natural resources against the wishes and interests of local peoples, and even in the violent subversion of legitimate democratic protest (the tragic hunting down and eventual killing of Ken Saro Wiwa who led local opposition to environmental abuses by Royal Dutch Shell in Nigeria is a case in point).

Studies of the political effects of the accelerated globalization of the world economy consequent upon financial and trading deregulation indicate that globalization is undermining the sovereignty of the state, and diminishing the capacity of local communities and constitutive groups in civil society, such as labour unions and environmental protection groups, to resist the unfair exploitation of their labour and even that of their children, and the wanton destruction of local environments (Hirst and Thompson, 1996).

Even if foreign direct investment could be regulated in ways which did not subvert democracy, unjustly exploit local labour, and destroy environments (a subject to which we shall return) it is still the case that most of this investment is not going to the impoverished and highly indebted countries of Africa and Latin America. They need protection, and special treatment, in the global trading environment if they are to establish local markets for locally produced goods and services and so end their debilitating dependency on the vagaries of primary commodity prices, and become more attractive locations for direct investment.

In the nineteenth century, when Britain's cotton industry was threatened by the high quality and competitive price of Indian cotton, the British colonial government used tariffs to favour cotton factories in Lancashire and Yorkshire over cotton work-shops in Calcutta and Bombay. When white settlers in New England wanted to cut the apron strings of the colonial power and protest at the unfairness of British tariffs and protectionism, they dumped British imported goods in the harbour at Boston in what became known as the Boston Tea Party. They eventually erected tariff barriers of their own against imported goods, just as Britain had done to imports from New England. Similarly the new industrialized countries of East Asia established their economies through a mix of state planning, investment in people and protection for local production through tariff barriers and other mechanisms.

But, as we have seen, structural adjustment and the Uruguay Round disallow to the poorest economies of the South the essential mechanisms of tariffs and quotas which were used in the North to establish strong indigenous economies. Even worse, after powerful lobbying of the Uruguay Round of the Global Agreement on Tariffs and Trade by North America and the European Union in particular, GATT legitimized the con-tinuation of many quotas and tariffs in the USA and the EU, and some in East Asia and Japan, including the European Multi-Fibre Agreement which limits textile imports from the South. The Uruguay Round also permitted European Union quotas on car imports, tariffs and other restrictions on imported food, and substantial agricultural subsidies in the EU and North America. This has created a situation where Europe and North America can dump subsidized wheat, maize or rice on African or Latin American food markets, thus undermining the incomes of local farmers and producers, while still restricting the import and sale in the North of competitively priced manufactured goods, textiles or foodstuffs from low-wage developing economies in the South. At the same time countries in the South are forced by structural adjustment programmes, and the terms of the Uruguay Round, to abandon protection of their own agricultural and textile sectors and nascent manufacturing industries.

According to classical economists such as Mateus Ricardo, free trade advanced the collective sum of economic welfare because it allowed regions and towns within nation states to specialize in things they were good at or best situated to produce, which they could then trade at a comparative advantage with the things they were less suited to make and which others could make more cheaply. But the classical dogma of comparative advantage was conceived on the model of trade between traders and local communities within one political entity or nation. It only works on an international scale where there is some degree of equivalence of economic strength between the trading countries (such as exists within the European Union or between the States of the United States), and where sovereign nation states (or federations of states in the case of the EU and the USA) regulate, and therefore benefit from, manufacturing and trading activities.

In most colonial and post-colonial contexts, 'free' trade has been conducted under conditions of coercion and the threat of force. Comparative advantage has rarely been realized on both sides. Structural adjustment and the Uruguay Round are just the latest post-colonial examples of this kind of coercion, forcing labour and environmental deregulation, as well as financial and trade deregulation, on the economies of the South (though not on the economies of the North). The principal beneficiaries of this global injustice are the multinational corporations based in the North who control an ever-growing proportion of global trade. As a consequence of adjustment nascent manufacturing plants in the South have frequently closed in the face of a flood of subsidized foreign imports while that which poor nations have left to sell – cheap labour and natural resources – is mobilized at levels which are producing social and environmental chaos, chaos which is then blamed on the ungovernability or tribalism of post-colonial peoples. The unequal flows of foreign direct investment offer no effective panacea to this situation.

The deregulation of trade and global markets, like the Keynesian dogma of the advantages of public debt, represents the application of an economic dogma which is clearly disadvantaging the poorest, only this time it is being applied with the force of a new international legal and juridical body, the World Trade Organization. As with the rules of international debt and structural adjustment, the current rules of deregulated free trade and finance offer no realistic hope that the poorest countries and communities of Africa, Latin America and South Asia can escape their impoverishment and begin to establish strong local economies which can compete on an equal footing in world markets.

Ideas for reform of the international trading system are not hard to find (see Chapters 6 and 7). Once again it is the resistance of the governments of the rich nations of the North, and of the World Trade Organization, which has to be overcome by democratic pressure if proposed reforms are ever to come into effect. Without such reforms, 'free' trade and globalization will continue to be covert language for a global economic process whereby the natural resources and labour power of poor nations are expropriated by rich nations, and in particular by the principal economic actors of rich nations, including the World Bank, the IMF, the World Trade Organization, multinational corporations and transnational banks.

Idolatry, Trade and the Economy of the Gift

The ban on idolatry occupies a central place in the Ten Commandments in the Hebrew Bible where idolatry is understood as the worship of created things in the place of God. Oscar Romero, the assassinated Archbishop of San Salvador, wrote that idolatry offends God and destroys human beings (Romero, 1998). The idols that he judged were oppressing the people of El Salvador were those of wealth, private property and national security. The inordinate love of these things was, in Romero's view, the principal cause of the suffering and poverty of the people. The Archbishop identified the militarization, repression and violence of Central American society (such as the violence experienced by unionists on banana plantations in Costa Rica) as the outcome of the idolization of wealth, the powerful using violence to protect their property, and to acquire more. He experienced the violence of idolatry in his own body for he was gunned down in his cathedral in San Salvador while saying Mass because his preaching and writing threatened the accumulated power and wealth of the landowning families who controlled El Salvador.

According to the liberation theologian Jon Sobrino, who also lives in El Salvador, the idols of wealth, private property and militarization are 'divinities of death' in Latin America which, like the Inca gold sought by the Conquistadors, generate death through impoverishment and violence (Sobrino, 1994). They acquire transcendent and ultimate power by taking on the 'trappings of divinity'; they become self-justifying, unquestionable, untouchable. The contemporary manifestation of these divine trappings is the economic structuring of society and the organization of international capitalism which 'produce millions of innocent victims, whom they despatch to the slow death of hunger and the violent death of repression' (Sobrino, 1994).

This analysis of idolatry is rooted in the context of the experience of oppression in Latin America. It is also rooted in the Bible. The compilers of the Torah (the first five books of the Hebrew Bible), like the Hebrew prophets, condemned the gods of the Canaanites such as Moloch and Baal because the worship of their images involved rebellion against Yahweh who was lord of all creation. The cults of these gods required human sacrifices and the exposing of infants, practices which Romero saw mirrored in the repression of the poor and the deaths of their malnourished children. Sobrino also points out the parallels in the Hebrew Prophets:

> According to the prophets, it is useless to put one's trust in idols, actualized in foreign powers and wealth, but furthermore – and this is the decisive point – these idols

produce victims: orphans, widows, refugees, the poor, the weak, the miserable ... victims whom God calls 'my' people in Isaiah and Micah. These victims are the evidence of the evil of the idols, not just their inability to save their adherents. And this is the objective reason for not adoring other gods: because their reality is essentially the contrary to the reality of the Lord. If the Lord produces life, the others produce death. (Sobrino, 1994)

Sobrino also indicates the parallels between the theological critique of idolatry in Latin America and St Paul's exposition of sin and idolatry in Romans 1.18–32:

The original fault is not simply not to know God, but to suppress the truth through wickedness (v. 18), which leads to a specific negation of God: exchanging the truth of God for lies and so adoring creatures rather than God (v. 25). The results of this idolization of creatures are their own dehumanization (vv. 26ff) and outward conduct that, in our terms, makes victims of others: wickedness, evil, covetousness, malice, envy, murder, strife ... (vv. 29ff). (Sobrino, 1994)

On this analysis, the oppression of the poor in banana plantations in Costa Rica or coffee plantations in El Salvador is a manifestation not only of an economic effect or of social disorder. It is a spiritual problem, the product of the denial of the God of life. The question of the poor, according to Sobrino, is fundamentally the question of God, and of what kind of God we worship.

The Israelites were called out and rescued from slavery in order to become a holy people who worshipped Yahweh and who sought to live according to the laws of God which directed them to a moral and social order quite distinct from surrounding cultures. Israelite society was marked off from its neighbours by a preference for equality over extremes of wealth and poverty, by not requiring the exposure of infants or other human sacrifices, and by its opposition to debt and bonded slavery.

Christians are similarly called to follow the God who in Jesus Christ condemned the worship of mammon as the complete opposite to the worship of God. Just as Jesus condemned the love of money, he also promised life and justice to the poor who were its victims: 'I came that they may have life, and have it abundantly' (John 10.10). The materiality of this abundant life is revealed in miracles of healing, and of feeding hungry crowds. It is revealed most completely in the bodily resurrection of Jesus. The resurrection demonstrated in the material world that the redemption of life from sin and evil is not deferred into some invisible and incorporeal spiritual future. On the contrary, the God who was in Christ crucified is the God who is in Jesus Christ risen from the dead, walking and talking with his disciples, breaking bread with them, sharing a meal of fish on the beach with them, and sending them into the world by the power of the Spirit to turn the established order of things upside down. The bodily resurrection of Jesus Christ anticipates and brings near the restoration of the original order and abundance of creation itself.

The Genesis creation stories describe the abundance of life experienced by the earliest humans, and represent life in all its diversity as the gift of God. The covenant which is made between Yahweh and the Hebrews is designed to restore this creational abundance in the midst of a land 'flowing with milk and honey' which itself is God's gift to God's people. And the exchange of gifts is central to the covenant God makes with the people of Israel. Jacob makes a gift covenant with God: 'Of all that you give me I will surely give one-tenth to you' (Genesis 28.20–2). The Deuteronomist establishes the ritual of the first fruits as a central act of worship whose liturgy included the following words:

'A wandering Aramean was my ancestor; he went down into Egypt and lived there as an alien, few in number, and there he became a great nation, mighty and populous. When the Egyptians treated us harshly and afflicted us, by imposing hard labour on us, we cried to the Lord, the God of our ancestors; the Lord heard our voice and saw our affliction, our toil, and our oppression. The Lord brought us out of Egypt with a mighty hand and an outstretched arm, with a terrifying display of power, and with signs and wonders; and he brought us into this place, and gave us this land, a land flowing with milk and honey. So now I bring the first of the fruit of the ground that you, O Lord, have given me.' You shall set it down before the Lord your God and bow down before the Lord your God. Then you, together with the Levites and the aliens who reside among you, shall celebrate with all the bounty that the Lord your God has given to you and to your house. (Deuteronomy 26.5–11)

The power of God in rescuing and redeeming the people of Israel was affirmed every time the people of Israel offered up the first fruits of the land. And every time they celebrated the fecundity of the land, they praised the God who gave them the land which prospered them.

It was the anthropologist Marcel Mauss who first pointed out the central role of gift-giving in the earliest forms of human economic and exchange activity (Mauss, 1990). In modern market societies we tend to contrast the giving of gifts as a voluntary or free form of exchange with market activity and trading which is controlled by contract and monetary equivalence. However, Mauss argued that in archaic societies gift-giving involved honour and generosity, and created the obligation to give in return, and that this was the case whether the gifts were given to people or offered to God.

Seen in this light, the Israelite ritual of the first fruits involved an act of giving which invited divine reciprocation: so long as the first fruits were offered up to God, the land would retain its abundance. Similarly, the burning of sacrifices on the altar is both required by God as obligation, and in turn was felt to bind God to the continuing welfare of God's people. And so when the people of Israel offered sacrifices to idols, who did not gift the land to them, the prophets argued that it was their own actions which caused the land to lose its fertility and ultimately the loss of the land through conquest and exile.

Mauss's insight about the connection between gift-giving, exchange, duty and obligation helps us to understand what is wrong with the present pattern and rules of the global trading economy. In the ancient and primal gift economy, gifts are exchanged in order to establish relationships of respect and care, and to create and affirm solidarity between those who exchange the gifts. The exchange of gifts buys peace with neighbours and peace with God. It also has another vital social function, which is the prevention of extremes of wealth and poverty. The one who has more or acquires more through fortune or hard work is also required to share more generously with everyone else. The hunter who is one day lucky in his hunting shares the food with his neighbours and not just his blood relatives. On other days others will be lucky and he and his household will then not go hungry.

Mauss gives the example of the Native American potlatch, when large quantities of animal skins, beads, food and drink were brought together, exchanged, consumed and even destroyed, as an essential means of wealth distribution which maintained equality in the tribe, while also gaining honour for those who gave most generously. Almsgiving also has the same function:

> Alms are the fruits of a moral notion of the gift and of fortune on the one hand, and of a notion of sacrifice, on the other. Generosity is an obligation, because Nemesis avenges the poor and the gods for superabundance of happiness and wealth of certain people who should rid themselves of it. This is the ancient morality of the gift which has become a principle of justice. The gods and the spirits accept that the share of wealth and happiness that has been offered to them and had been hitherto destroyed in useless sacrifices should serve the poor and children. In recounting this we are recounting the history of the moral ideas of the Semites. The Arab *sedaka* originally meant exclusively justice, as did the Hebrew *zedaqa*: it has come to mean alms. (Mauss, 1990)

These observations shed an intriguing light on the whole philosophy underlying the creation of organizations of international aid such as Oxfam, Save the Children and Christian Aid.

But Mauss is making an even more profound point and one which is directly relevant to the way in which the current rules of global trade are damaging the poor. The exchange of gifts is an exchange which creates obligation and involves reciprocity. It is designed to keep the wealth of nature, transformed into material goods which meet human needs and aspirations, in circulation. It recognizes a deep morality and spirit which is involved in the circulation of goods. The ancients believed that when nature's abundance was hoarded this abundance would dry up. Equally, where individuals failed to honour the obligations created in receiving gifts or in experiencing good fortune, wealth was in danger of becoming a fetish or idol, and of subverting the network of relationships, and the fertility of nature, which were, and are, both involved in wealth creation which benefits the whole society.

This of course is precisely what is happening through the processes of commodification which are making so many poor in the contemporary global economy. The offerings of people's, and even children's, sweated labour, of a nation's precious and irreplaceable tropical forest, fishing grounds, or minerals, are traded in the global market place for money-values which come nowhere near compensating for the cost and sacrifice of that which is traded. Exchanges involving the denial of human dignity, such as that experienced by Eldora Fuentes and her family on the plantation in Costa Rica, have become common-place under the rules of the current trading system between poor and rich nations and their corporations and bankers. Such exchanges are a denial of the common humanity of producer, trader and consumer. Unlike the exchange systems of ancient societies, they subvert human solidarity, and destroy the abundance of nature's gifts.

In the Bible, intercultural trade and regional exchange of nature's abundance, and of the fruits of human work, are not seen as intrinsically evil nor as contrary to the divine intention for creation as revealed in the Old and New Testaments. In the Book of Kings we read how the Queen of Sheba graces the courts of Solomon with many wonderful gifts which are in turn reciprocated. International interdependence through trade and exchange is an ancient practice and when conducted fairly it has the potential to bring the peoples of the world together in a solidarity which advances world peace, and destroys the roots of war. The abolition of international trade will not of itself advance the conditions of the poor, nor hopes for a more peaceful world.

What is condemned in the law and the prophets, and in the New Testament writings, is not trade *per se* but unjust trading, exchanges which do not give measure for measure, and hoarding by the rich at the expense of the poor. Amos explicitly condemned unjust trading practices (Amos 5). Ezekiel condemns the exchange of human beings for merchandise such as ivory tusks, embroidered cloth and rubies, and excess trade in luxury goods and the instruments of war (Ezekiel 27.13–27). Jesus condemned exchanges, tithes and taxes which imposed excessive burdens on the poor. Reflecting the law codes of the Hebrew Bible, Jesus taught the importance of reciprocity and generosity in gift-giving: 'You received without payment; give without payment' (Matthew 10.8). The parable of the talents contrasts favourably those who put their gift of talents to work and into circulation with the one who hides them away in a hole in the ground. Similarly, the man who planned to hoard the abundant crops from his large estates in new and bigger barns died and came under judgement before he could enjoy his hoarded wealth (Luke 12.16–20).

It is not the abolition but the regulation and reform of world trade which is urgently required to improve the position of the world's poor. Fair trade and aid organizations in both North and South are campaigning for new rules of international trade which outlaw child labour, which prevent companies from terrorizing unionists, which disallow the fire-sale of irreplaceable natural assets like tropical forests, and which allow poor nations as well as rich ones to use tariffs, quotas and other measures to protect local food markets, fragile environments, and emergent and essential industries, such as textiles and construction, from unfair competition. In the following chapters we will see how the proper regulation of international finance by sovereign governments and democratic reform of the World Trade Organization, combined with codes of conduct on multinational corporations, and ethical consumerism and ethical investment, have the potential to create a fairer global economic order in which the labour and lands of the poor are traded in ways which affirm the common humanity of all nations, and the interdependent ecology of the planet.

Sources

Lucy Alexander and Emma Donlan (1977), 'Testimonies Taken From Banana Workers in Costa Rica', Christian Aid, Internal Briefing Paper

Edward Goldsmith (1996), 'Free Trade and the Environment' in Jerry Mander and Edward Goldsmith (eds.), *The Case Against the Global Economy: And For a Turn Toward the Local* (San Francisco: Sierra Book Clubs)

Paul Hirst and Graham Thompson (1996), *Globalization in Question: The International Economy and Possibilities of Governance* (Cambridge: Polity Press)

Michael Jacobs (1996), *The Politics of the Real World: Meeting the New Century* (London: Earthscan)

Matthew Lockwood (1997), 'Closer Together, Further Apart: A Discussion Paper on Globalisation' (London: Christian Aid)

Marcel Mauss (1990), *The Gift: The Form and Reason for Exchange in Archaic Societies* (New Eng. trans., London: Routledge)

Michael Northcott (1996), *The Environment and Christian Ethics* (Cambridge: Cambridge University Press)

Michael Northcott (1998) *Urban Theology: A Reader* (London: Cassell)

Oscar Romero (1998), *The Violence of Love* (Eng. trans., Farmington, PA: Plough Publications)

Jon Sobrino (1994), 'The Question of God: God of Life and Idols of Death', Excursus 2 in Jon Sobrino, *Jesus the Liberator: A Historical-Theological Reading of Jesus of Nazareth* (Eng. trans., Maryknoll, NY: Orbis)

World Bank (1992), *Development and the Environment* (Oxford: Oxford University Press)

Organizations

The current head of the World Trade Organization is:

Renato Ruggiero World Trade Organization, Geneva, Switzerland
http://www.wto.org/
Fax: 41 22 739 5458

The following organizations are actively campaigning for the reform
of the World Trade Organization:

Focus on the Global South c/o CUSRI, Wisit Prachuabmoh
Building, Chulalongkorn University, Phyathai Rd, Bangkok 10330,
Thailand
Tel: 66 2 218 7363
Fax: 66 2 255 9976
E-mail: admin@focusweb.org
Website: http://www.focusweb.org
Contact: Walden Bello

World Development Movement 25 Beehive Place, London SW9 9QR
Tel: 0800 328 2153
Fax: 0171 738 6098
E-mail: wdm@wdm.org.uk
Website: www.wdm.org.uk

4 The Priority of Debt Remission

A Charge on the Poorest of the Poor in Debt-Burdened Tanzania

Our village, Mavala, is in the mountains in the west of Tanzania. We get long, hard winters and the red-brown soil is poor and there is not much water around here. The land has been worked too hard for a long time. We are all farmers and plots get smaller over the generations because they are passed down from fathers to their sons. We mostly grow maize, and some wheat and beans. We also have some cows but not many these days. The price we get for our crops is very low and we need all the money we can get for school and hospital fees, and for local government tax which has gone up a lot though we get so few services from them. We used not to have to pay fees but Tanzania has become very poor because of the government debt and all the social services now cost a lot of money.

I am a village health worker and all the time I am seeing what poverty is doing to people here. Many of the children here have kwashiorkor, the disease of malnutrition. We don't get much protein from our diet which is mainly maize and beans, and we can't afford meat or fish which we used to eat with it. I visited a family yesterday and their little girl, who is not quite three years old, was badly malnourished; she had a distended stomach and terribly thin limbs, and she no longer wants to eat. She is very seriously ill and might die, even though her mother is on a health programme from the village clinic. The child needs a regular intake of milk, eggs, and fish or meat to pick up but they possess only a few chickens. They have very little money and grew only enough maize for the family to eat, and not enough to sell. What money her husband manages to make, selling beer at the village social centre, all goes on school fees and clothes.

Like many families here, both parents are out during the day working the fields and trying to make ends meet with some kind of small business or a job in a faraway town. The small children are left at home on their own, or with their brothers and sisters, and eating the leftovers from the maize meal from the night before.

At least their father lives at home. Many of the men have been forced to leave the village to try to find work in towns miles away. Even when they grow enough crops to sell a surplus on their *shamba* (the family land) they get a very low price from the traders who sell in Dar es Salaam at five times the price they pay to us.

Today I visited the hospital in Milo and I heard about a young woman from our village who died there only last week. She had left the village to find work in Njombe town and ended up working in a bar, and fell into prostitution. She died from AIDS, though we don't say that in the village but everyone knows. It has been getting worse recently. So many young people go to the towns because life is so poor and their families are unable to feed them here in the village. But when they get to the towns they cannot find work, and there is a lot of crime, and a growing drug problem. It never used to be like this but in the last few years so many jobs have been lost even in the biggest industries, like clothing. Nyerere used to protect Tanzanian industry but now anyone can import into Tanzania and lots of second-hand clothes from Europe are sold here, which is destroying our own clothes industry.

The women really suffer because of the hospital fees. When they are going to have a baby, the women are afraid to go to the hospital until they are in labour because they cannot afford the charges. Then it is too far to walk so they have the baby at home, sometimes with only their family to help them as there are so few birth attendants to go round all the villages. Also when they or their children get sick, people just go and buy some cheap pills from the shop in the hope they will make them better. Often they get worse and then when they do go to the clinic they are already hospital cases. And the hospital is not so good, just a tin roof and bricks, with the cold wind blowing through. Parents have to stay with their children though there is nowhere for them to sleep, or if it is the parents who are sick, they need another relative to cook their food and take care of them. Malaria is still a real problem here. But children are now dying of common complaints like diarrhoea. One child from the village died in Milo hospital a few weeks ago from dysentery. The mother had tried to treat him at home with some cheap medicine from the village shop. The village clinic refused to treat him when she took him there. It is 20 kilometres on a dirt track to the hospital and by the time she got him there he was too far gone and died in the night.

As a village health worker I try to teach people about sanitation and nutrition. Clean water is piped to the village thanks to a project funded by the church and some money from overseas. The villagers dug 8 kilometres of trenches for the pipes. But some of the houses are a long way from the six outlets and so the women still spend an hour or more every day carrying water. We particularly appreciate visits from Mrs Ngaio who runs the community health care programme. She has brought seeds for things like Chinese leaves and other green vegetables. We planted these on our vegetable plot so we can distribute them when they are grown. We were given a cockerel and three other families got one as well. People are not used to looking after their cockerels so Mrs Ngaio gave a seminar on taking care of them. They need to be kept indoors if they are not to die from diseases they pick up around the village, and they need to be fed properly and not just left to eat rubbish. We now have twenty-two chicks and we will soon be able to have enough eggs to sell in the village.

Like most people, we farm a *shamba* but it is hard to find the money for fertilizer and pesticide. Without these you can't grow crops properly, the maize all gets eaten by weevils and whenever we plant the crops do not grow well. Even basic household items like salt and soap have been going up in price and yet the price we get for any surplus maize and beans is still very low. Also we do not have enough money for the children's education. We now have to pay for education. The school fees are often raised. Sometimes people send their children to school and they come home again because the fees have gone up. People think they have found the money for the term, and then they haven't. Our daughter Lydia is nine and she still has not started school. She really wants to go but we needed her to look after her baby brother Amoniche who is now nearly two. We will send her to school in November. Our older boys are both behind in their schooling because we could not send them at the right time also because of the fees. Fadhile is eleven and he misses class a lot because he is in a class with much younger children and he is embarrassed to be there. He has lost interest in school and we have no hope anyway of being able to send him to secondary school. It is 25 kilometres from here and even if we could afford the fees we cannot afford the lodging for him. The future is very bleak. We are still in a condition of poverty and I do not see much hope that our children can escape this.

Towards Debt Forgiveness

There are 50 children in Mavala village who should be at school but whose parents cannot afford to send them (Spray, 1997). There are many who are severely malnourished, and the child mortality rate in Tanzania has been increasing inexorably over the last ten years. At the same time Tanzania, like most of sub-Saharan Africa, is in the grip of an AIDS epidemic. In Uganda, one quarter of women attending a maternity clinic are infected with AIDS. Drug treatment for AIDS is a dream for most people in Tanzania, and little money is available for a pro-gramme of prevention. Many cannot afford the drugs to treat their children when they get malaria.

Until 1982, when Tanzania came under the external direction of the economists of the International Monetary Fund, school-ing and medical treatment were free. Tanzania first got into difficulties in the late 1970s. The causes are primarily external, though internal factors played a part. In the 1970s the socialist economy achieved a growth rate of 5 per cent. However in the 1980s and 1990s this shrank to less than 3 per cent. Prominent among the external causes of Tanzania's economic crisis was declining terms of trade. As Julius Nyerere pointed out in 1982: 'To buy a 7 ton truck in 1981 we had to produce and sell abroad about four times as much cotton, or three times as much cashew or three times as much coffee, or ten times as much tobacco as we had to produce and sell in 1976/77' (Cheru, 1989).

Rising oil prices, declining agricultural and raw material prices, and the recession in the West all contributed to a major decline in Tanzania's foreign exchange earnings. At the same time Tanzania had to cope with the immense burden of military intervention in Uganda which increased Tanzania's external debt (Tetzlaff, 1991). These problems were exacerbated by poor domestic economic management. The government collectivized agricultural production, and also nationalized and tried to expand the industrial sector which, combined with rigid import controls, had the effect of suppressing both agricultural and industrial production (Tetzlaff, 1991). Climatic threats to agricultural production also played their part in the early to mid-eighties.

Tanzania's external debt stood at $7,802 million in 1995. With a population of 29.6 million and a per capita gross national product of $640, Tanzania is one of the ten poorest countries in the world and it has one of the highest debt per head ratios of any poor indebted country (Tetzlaff, 1991). The consequences of the debt for the people of Tanzania have been devastating. As the General Secretary of the Anglican Church in Tanzania comments, 'Their life has become intolerable and I can also say that the debt burden is killing people because people cannot afford to go to hospital. If they don't have drugs, they die. It is a direct result of the debt crisis' (Duckworth, 1997).

Tanzania's problems are a microcosm of the mushrooming debt crisis throughout sub-Saharan Africa whose debt burden has grown four times between 1982 and the present, despite the imposition of strict economic austerity programmes designed to cut public spending and release funds for debt repayment.

As a consequence of the debt crisis, sub-Saharan Africa, the poorest and most underdeveloped region on earth, pays to governments and banks in the rich North $12.6 billion a year, or $24 million every day, in debt service payments. And for every dollar the region receives in aid from the North, the region pays 11 dollars to the North in debt repayment. In most years the International Monetary Fund takes out more from the region in debt repayments than it puts into the region in the form of new loans. In 1991 the surplus it extracted from sub-Saharan Africa in its operations was $600 million.

The United Nations Children's Fund estimates that $9.6 billion – less than one year's debt servicing payments – spent on health, education, clean water and sanitation would be enough to save the lives of the vast majority of the millions of children who die in sub-Saharan Africa from preventable diseases and malnutrition. And it is this very high rate of child mortality which is the principal reason why African parents have so many children. When child mortality is so high, and children are parents' only security for their own old age, then rational parents will choose to have more children.

Much creative thinking was given by economists to the debt crisis in the 1980s, especially since Mexico threatened to default on loans in 1982 which it owed primarily to North American banks. The principal mechanism they came up with was rescheduling. The International Monetary Fund agrees a new payment schedule between the 'Paris Club' of lending nations and the debtor country, and on the basis of this agreement advances new funds, which are added to the existing loans, in order to meet interest payments on these loans. But rescheduling is no solution. All it does is defer the problem of repayment to a later date, while the new loans and new loan interest are added to the principal of the earlier loans. The banks and agencies involved in rescheduling also charge a percentage of the amount owed as a fee for the rescheduling arrangement which further increases the quantity of debt, and the size of monthly debt repayments, with each rescheduling deal (Kote-Nioki, 1996).

In recognition of this, the influential Harvard economist

Jeffrey Sachs, the architect of structural adjustment, argues that debtor and creditor countries both have interests in moving towards debt reduction rather than debt rescheduling (Sachs, 1989). Noting that the 1980s attempts to reschedule and partially write-off debt had resulted in large net outflows of funds from debtor countries to creditor countries which were subverting any chance of economic uplift, Sachs contends that debt reduction is the only logical route.

Sachs enumerates the principal arguments against debt reduction as follows: in the long term, with sufficient economic growth, all indebted countries will be able to repay their debts; debt forgiveness will undermine the world financial system; debt forgiveness involves a moral hazard whereby the imprudent or corrupt misuse of borrowed money by debtor countries is effectively rewarded. In response to these arguments Sachs points out that the huge size of external debts, and the large number of parties owed money, make it impossible to organize indebted economies back into a position of economic recovery. Even if at some point in the future indebted countries might be able to begin to pay off the principal of the loans, Sachs notes that most of them will not be able to do this for many years. He points out that without debt reduction, bad economic performance is actually rewarded as larger budget deficits, or reduced tax revenues, reduce the amount of debt repayment required while economic success is rewarded with higher debt repayments. Sachs also argues that, since it was corrupt military dictators who obtained and misused the debt, while more democratic governments are being punished with debt repayment, debt reduction will not reward past bad behaviour. Finally, regarding the purported threat to the world financial system, Sachs notes that since debt reduction will be funded from public money, the main problem is not that the world economy is threatened but that taxpayers' money is being used to reward the poor lending decisions of bankers and development 'experts'.

Sachs' arguments for debt reduction and forgiveness are based on a recognition of mutual self-interest between North and South. The inability of southern economies to repay their debts means reduced markets for northern manufacturers in southern economies. It also means that public infrastructural investments and maintenance are declining, with consequent knock-on effects on northern-financed investment projects in the South. Resolving the debt crisis would also reduce the 'boomerang' effect of pressures on the North which, as we have seen, include economic migrants, mafioso capitalism and increased global trade in narcotics.

There are currently three forms of debt reduction for old debt on offer from the Paris Club. The first and largest kind of debt reduction is straightforward debt forgiveness. Germany has led the way in this approach. Since 1978 it has forgiven $5.6 billion of debt owed to the German government by the poorest countries, including a number in sub-Saharan Africa (OECD, 1997). The United States has only forgiven debt where debt forgiveness has served its strategic and foreign policy objectives. Thus Egypt was let off its debt to the US government of just under $10 billion as reward for helping the United States in the Gulf War. Poland was released from its debt to the US of $2.7 billion as reward for being the first nation in Eastern Europe to break with the Soviet bloc. The British government has forgiven $2 billion of old debt, mostly for nations in sub-Saharan Africa. In total more than $18 billion of government-to-government debt has been forgiven since 1991.

The second approach is debt conversion. This approach involves three kinds of conversion, inaugurated in the Brady Initiative of 1989. One involves converting debt owed as foreign currency into local currency which is then used to purchase equity in a local business or to fund a development project. Under this approach, $2 billion of debt has been converted (OECD, 1997). Another kind of debt conversion involves debt buy-back where indebted countries buy back their debt from commercial banks with funds provided by northern governments or the World Bank. They buy the debt back at a discount and are then given a longer period to repay it. In this way, $2.5 billion of debt owed to commercial banks has been converted. The third kind of debt conversion is 'debt-for-nature swaps'. Again the funds involved have been small – around $3 billion –

but the idea is that debt is converted into environmental programmes to protect threatened habitats, such as coral reefs around some islands in the Philippines, or the protection of the few remaining undamaged forest areas in Madagascar (FAO, 1993).

Debt conversion schemes have been much criticized. They are seen as a new form of colonialism where foreign creditors acquire ownership of local industry under debt-for-equity swaps or of land areas designated as environmental reserves under debt-for-nature swaps. Debt conversion has also not been effective in reducing the outstanding amount owed by indebted nations significantly. Chile and Bolivia were the single largest recipients of debt-for-equity conversion in the 1980s, but their debt remained at damagingly high levels (Larrain and Velasco, 1990). Costa Rica did rather better. In 1989, two-thirds of its $1.5 billion debt was converted, and effectively written off. However, there is a suspicion that most debt conversion schemes, which involve only a small fraction of indebted country debts, are more to do with rhetoric than reality. They give the appearance that Western governments and international financial institutions are actively working to reduce debt, but in reality debt is mostly not reduced but moved from one lender to another and the payments deferred, while the interest continues to build up. In sub-Saharan Africa, where the debt is largest and such a major cause of human suffering and of economic and political instability, debt conversion schemes are not likely to make any significant impact (African Centre for Monetary Studies, 1992).

The latest debt reduction scheme, drawn up by the Paris Club, the International Monetary Fund and the World Bank in 1995, is the Highly Indebted Poor Country Initiative (HIPC). This initiative is intended to allow for debt reduction for countries which have demonstrated a consistent record of financial austerity and economic liberalization as prescribed under structural adjustment programmes. Uganda was the first country to become eligible for debt write-off through the HIPC scheme in 1997, but under pressure from Japan, which at $83.7 billion holds the largest single tranche of indebted poor country debt, debt reduction for Uganda has been deferred at the time of writing. In principle, under the HIPC, members of the Paris Club of creditor nations have agreed to provide up to 80 per cent debt forgiveness for countries which meet the economic criteria (OECD, 1997). However, the total value of the HIPC, which is only directed at commercial and government lending, and not at monies owed to the World Bank and the International Monetary Fund, is estimated at only $6 billion as compared to indebted poor country total debt in respect of commercial and government lending of $203 billion in 1998.

Despite all the palliatives offered by the Paris Club, and the adjustment measures imposed by the World Bank and the International Monetary Fund, the total debt burden for sub-Saharan Africa, including commercial, government and international financial institution debt, continues to grow. Between 1980, before the commencement of rescheduling and adjustment programmes, and 1994 it grew from $80 billion to $313 billion. The lack of effectiveness of these successive programmes for debt relief is seen by many non-Western economists as evidence of a deeper agenda in debt negotiations. As the African economist Fantu Cheru notes, the aim does not seem to be to relieve debt but rather to increase the exposure of African countries to cheap Western imports, and their reliance on Western aid and continuing financial packages (Cheru, 1989). In other words, the debt crisis is viewed as a new form of colonization in Africa.

It is against this picture of growing debt, and of measures supposedly designed to reduce debt which actually increase it, that the Jubilee 2000 Coalition, together with many non-governmental organizations and church leaders in North and South, and past and present Secretaries of the United Nations, propose a new and radical solution to the growing debt crisis – debt forgiveness. The Jubilee 2000 proposal links debt relief to the coming of the third millennium in the year 2000, and to the Jubilee principle in the Hebrew Bible.

The Jubilee 2000 plan involves two basic principles. A poor country is defined as a country with an income per head of less than $3,500, with countries with less than $2,000 per head getting additional special treatment. Poor country debt is defined as unpayable on three separate measures: when it exceeds annual national income by 50 per cent, when it exceeds the value of exports by 200 per cent, and when it is more than 200 per cent of government revenues (Spray, 1997). Under the Jubilee 2000 proposal, debts defined in these terms as unpayable would be paid off by a combination of government aid from northern countries, tax write-offs where debt is still owed to commercial banks, and mobilization of International Monetary Fund gold reserves. The sale of these reserves would realize around $40 billion. They are not needed to support currency values, nor are they used for other purposes: they were conferred on the International Monetary Fund at the end of the Second World War to give it international financial standing. Estimates of the cost of the Jubilee 2000 proposal are approximate but it is said to be roughly $100 billion spread over three or four years. To put this figure in perspective, it is less than 0.5 per cent of the value of daily financial transactions on all global markets, and only four times the value of International Monetary Fund rescue packages in South East Asia in 1997–8.

Opponents of debt forgiveness argue, as we have seen, that it would reward bad behaviour, that it would threaten international financial order, and finally that it would allow formerly indebted governments to go out and contract new loans for more ill-conceived prestige development projects, for military spending or for the personal gain of government ministers. In response to these concerns, Jubilee 2000 argues that debt forgiveness would carry its own discipline. Lenders would be unlikely to advance further monies to countries which had effectively been declared bankrupt.

The key features of the Jubilee 2000 plan are as follows:

1. Poor countries are to be eligible for debt relief when they have an income per head of less than $3,500.
2. Unpayable debt, as defined above, is to be comprehensively written off, not rescheduled as in past debt relief schemes. This debt write-off is to be funded by the gold reserves of the

International Monetary Fund and the World Bank, by official
government aid from the countries of the North, and by tax
breaks in exchange for debt write-offs to those commercial
banks which have debt exposure in countries concerned.
Debt forgiveness on this scale will also require reforms to the
International Monetary Fund which currently does not have
internal procedures for debt write-off.

3. Each indebted country should be dealt with on a case-by-
case basis, instead of the blanket International Monetary
Fund-imposed debt 'reduction' packages of the past, and
proper representation of governmental and non-governmental agencies from debtor countries should be provided
for in the debt forgiveness negotiations.

4. Estimates of debt overhang must be realistic. In the past the
International Monetary Fund has relied on wildly optimistic
debt repayment scenarios, assuming levels of export and
government revenues which are not achievable, particularly
after structural adjustment conditions have enforced currency devaluation and increased unemployment (thus lowering government revenues twice over).

5. The partnership agreement with each country will include a
plan to indicate how the resources released from debt repayment will be used for poverty eradication. These plans
should be open to scrutiny both internally and with international partners. This assumes democratic transparency in
national budgeting which is a key mechanism to ensure
political leaders do not contract further unpayable debts in
the future.

In 1998, around 70,000 people gathered in Birmingham and
surrounded the conference of prime ministers and finance
ministers of the G7 with a human chain to symbolize the
chains which bind the poorest people on earth to the burden of
international debt. They called on the ministers of the G7 to
advance a fully funded debt relief programme in time for the
millennium. Sadly the response of the G7 was extremely muted.
The ministers were far more concerned with economic shocks to
northern economies arising from currency and share price falls

in East Asia where the governments and multinationals of the G7 have made considerable capital investments.

The muted response to the problems of debt repayment in sub-Saharan Africa, Latin America and South Asia seems to indicate that the G7 are only prepared to exercise economic and political leadership to safeguard the interests of northern capital, and not to use their considerable powers for the benefit of the poor in the South. However the campaign for debt relief continues among churches and non-governmental organizations in both North and South.

Christ in Africa, Lord of the Powers

The book of the Acts of the Apostles records the birth of African Christianity in the account of Philip's meeting with the chief treasurer of the Queen of Ethiopia which ended in his being baptized by the apostle. African churches, bishops and theologians such as Augustine and Athanasius gave significant leadership in the ancient Christian Church (Parratt, 1995). But the record of Christianity in recent history in Africa is deeply ambiguous. African Christian leaders meeting in 1976 towards the close of the colonial experience in Africa made the following statement on the role of Christianity in that tragic history:

> The Gospel was used as an agency for a softening of
> national resistance to the plunder by the foreigners and a
> domestication of the minds and cultures of the dominated
> converts. In fact, foreign powers often gave Christians a
> privileged position within their arrangements for the
> administration of the countries. In the process Christian
> teaching got badly tainted by the search for selfish gain of
> the peoples who called themselves Christians and exercised
> power in the name of emperors and spiritual rulers.
> (Parratt, 1995)

While Christian missionaries were among those who de-nounced slavery and the pillage of Africa's resources in colonial times, the European churches were nonetheless a significant arm of the colonial powers. Their mission compounds were outposts of European culture and society. African converts were encouraged to abandon their traditional village customs and their ancestors, in order to receive European medicine and education and to be baptized as Christians. Until independence, and even beyond, the mission churches in Africa remained dependent on European leadership, liturgies, cultural forms and theologies. And missionary theology was often of an other-worldly style which failed to engage with the social, economic and political oppression of Africans by Europeans (Parratt, 1995).

However, in the period since independence, the African churches have grown as never before. Africa today has more active Christians than any other continent in the world. Many African Christians now belong to African independent churches where Christian worship, spirituality and theology are deeply rooted in African culture and tradition. John Mbiti enumerates some of the names of these new churches as follows:

> 'Believed Power of Jesus Christ in Kenya', 'Children of God Regeneration Church', 'Church of the Power of Jesus Christ', 'Power of Jesus Around the World Church', 'Church of Saviour's', 'Wokofu (Salvation) African Church' (Mbiti, 1973)

The names of these new churches bear witness to a distinctive feature of African spirituality, and this is the dynamic conception of salvation and deliverance. As Mbiti comments:

> The Christian message found a well-established notion that God rescues people when all other help is exhausted, and that this rescue is primarily from material and physical dilemmas. God does not save because he is Saviour; rather, he becomes Saviour when he does save. The concept of saving is a dynamic one which is rooted in a particular moment of desperation. (Mbiti, 1973)

Mbiti finds that 'the chief preoccupation of African Christians is "redemption" from physical dilemmas' (Mbiti, 1973). Africans find in the Christian God a new 'high' God, or Almighty God, who is the personification of the power which creates and governs the whole cosmos and is above all other spirits and powers. In Jesus they find this God personified as the one who saves the poor and the needy, the crushed and the oppressed, the one who rescues them from physical threats, who protects them from harm and who heals them in body and soul. The dilemmas and threats from which they seek deliverance include threats to the physical body, threats to relationships in the household and the village, and threats to life itself in the form of famine, disease and even war.

One of the most striking features of African independent churches is the immediacy of this experience of redemption, expressed in the language of their hymns, in rituals of healing and deliverance, and in shared testimonies to the miraculous power of God in people's lived experience.

> Jesus is the human concentration of that divine power which heals the sick, casts out spirits, cleanses from sorcery and witchcraft, renews life, abolishes death, conquers and protects from all evil powers both human and cosmic. In effect the earthly ministry of Jesus, as directed to the physical needs of his audience, now spans two thousand years and becomes alive in African Christians. (Mbiti, 1973)

The most powerful and pervasive external threat to the bodies, households and villages of Africa today is the slavery to external debt and debt repayment to which so much of sub-Saharan Africa is subjected.

In traditional African society, the chief is seen as having sacred power over such external threats, acting as a channel of cosmic forces which ensure the well-being of the community and protect it against outside forces (Bediako, 1982). The chief acquires his power because he is said to sit on the throne of the ancestors, who are venerated in most African tribal cultures. African theologians interpret the Lordship of Jesus through the metaphors of chief and ancestor. Like the early Christians, Africans find in the gospel assurance that sovereignty over and in the world has passed to Jesus Christ. Jesus Christ in African experience is Chief of all the powers in his triumphant resurrection from death, and is the Ancestor of all ancestors when he walks among the dead during his three days in the tomb (Bediako, 1982).

The saving work of Christ is seen primarily through this metaphor of victory over the powers, a victory which establishes the Lordship of Jesus above all other earthly and spiritual powers:

> The Christian message brings Jesus as the one who fought victoriously against the forces of the devil, spirits, sickness, hatred, fear, and death itself. In each of these areas he is the victor, the one hope, the one example, the one conqueror: and this makes sense to African peoples, it draws their attention, and it is pregnant with meaning. It gives to their myths an absolutely new dimension. The greatest need among African peoples is to see, to know, and to experience Jesus Christ as the victor over the powers and forces from which Africa knows no means of deliverance. (Mbiti, 1972)

Elizabeth Amoah and Mercy Oduyoye make a similar observation from the perspective of African women, who often bear the greatest burden of oppression under the yoke of debt slavery:

> The Christ whom African women worship, honor, and depend on is the victorious Christ, knowing that evil is a reality. Death and life-denying forces are the experience of women, and so Christ, who countered these forces and who gave back her child to the widow of Nain, is the African woman's Christ. (Amoah and Oduyoye, 1988)

This African appropriation of the victory of Christ has a particular and precise bearing on one of the principal roots of the problem of external debt in Africa. This is the corruption and autocracy of many African heads of state, and their use of foreign funds for military or prestige projects which did not address the needs of the people. The victory of Christ over earthly powers undermines all earthly claims to sacred power whether of the tribal chief, the head of state, or the World Bank and the International Monetary Fund. The redemption which Christ's victory represents challenges not only wrong religion but wrong government and wrong relationships. 'The good news to Africa is that people and communities have to be willing to die to all that dehumanizes on both personal and corporate levels' (Amoah and Oduyoye, 1988).

As Amoah and Oduyoye recognize, the threats to life in Africa today are not just external in origin. They have a major internal dimension, as manifest in the fact that even while African governments and leaders cut spending on health, education and clean water under structural adjustment programmes, they manage to maintain military budgets, and to continue purchasing Western arms, with the help of new export-linked loans from Britain, the United States and other arms-producing countries. The militarization of Africa has actually been stimulated by the structural adjustment programmes of the International Monetary Fund and the World Bank. Austerity programmes require 'strong' leaders backed by military force as means to impose them on unwilling peoples.

Mbiti points out that a weakness of the traditional African emphasis on external threats, and on the interpretation of Jesus as Victor over the powers, is a corresponding underemphasis on sin and guilt (Mbiti, 1973). In the traditional African worldview, sin and guilt are strongly connected to community. Sin is that which threatens the harmony and welfare of the village and the household. Such sins required expiation in the form of animal sacrifices. But the gravest threat to the welfare of the contemporary African village is the corruption of political leaders, and the secrecy of bankers and government officials who enable them to fulfil their militaristic and prestigious ambitions by mortgaging the future income of their peoples. The sacrifices these sins call for are also live sacrifices, not of animals but of people and their children.

Kwame Bediako finds that the problems of corruption and of economic oppression are linked to political Messianism in post-independence Africa. He notes that many African leaders tend to surround their political office with sacred images, symbols and rituals, drawn from African traditional religions, with which they mystify and cement their hold over the people and their lands (Bediako, 1995). Thus President Maputo of Zaire, who ran up debts of $5 billion on behalf of his people, regularly presented himself as the chief above chiefs, dressed in the skins of leopards, and with a fetish stick in his hand.

The underlying issue according to Bediako is the spiritualization of power in African society. The problem originates in the location of power in the realm of the ancestors. This lends to the experience of power in Africa a spiritual distance and a capriciousness, both of which are characteristic of the exercise of power by modern African presidents and heads of state (Bediako, 1995). Modern leaders adopt the language of the ancestral chief, and of solidarity with the tribe, as a means to justify authoritarianism and the suppression of dissident voices. Traditional African society is deeply formed around village and tribal community, both past, ancestral and present. But when this village community is projected on to the nation state it promotes the one-party state and the all-powerful president or national leader.

Bediako suggests that African Christianity therefore has a vital role in the transformation of modern African political consciousness. Against the claim to sacred power of many of Africa's modern leaders, Christians set the ultimacy of the Kingdom of God and the Lordship of Jesus Christ. Christians too believe that authority derives from the transcendent realm, from the Lord of Lords and King of Kings. But the difference is that Christians see this authority as being exercised on behalf of God, and therefore accountable – accountable to the moral laws and commands of the Bible, and accountable to the living people of God, and not to the hidden voices of ancestors:

> The struggle for true democracy in Africa unavoidably involves making room for the 'way of Jesus', the way of non-dominating power, in the political arrangements under which members of society and nation will relate to one another. The mind of Jesus, as related to the questions of politics and power, is *not* a dominating mind, *not* a self-pleasing or self-asserting mind, but rather a saving mind, a redemptive mind, a servant mind (Bediako, 1995).

Bediako notes that Christian churches have been active in many African countries in the struggle for pluralism, human rights and democracy. In the same way the churches of Africa have been most vocal in condemning the slavery of debt, and in calling for debt remission. However, he notes that this call for debt remission is not made lightly. The churches and their leaders have frequently condemned, often at personal peril, the internal and external corruption and secrecy which have allowed such massive debts to build up in the first place, and to be used for purposes which are often contrary to the welfare of the peoples of Africa.

Should the debts be forgiven, it is vital that African political leaders are not again able to contract new debts without the active consent of their people, expressed in arrangements which guarantee popular scrutiny of national spending and budgetary plans. The Ugandan parliament has passed a law preventing government ministers from entering into any financial arrangements with external powers without first laying the plans before parliament for the scrutiny of the people. As we have seen, debt forgiveness of the kind proposed by Jubilee 2000 will also carry its own discipline which will help in the control of future debt. Countries which have a record of bad debt, and which have been forgiven large sums of debt, are less likely to attract new lending in the future.

If the sacrifices of Africa's peoples, and of their children, are to come to an end the power of debt in Africa must be dethroned, and the power of the external agencies which impose this debt on Africa must be challenged and overturned. The way of the Lordship of Jesus is not the way of military conquest or of dominating power. It is the way of servanthood and forgiveness. Christ has paid the debts of the peoples of Africa in his sacrifice on the cross. Debt forgiveness is not only the moral but the spiritual response which the desperate plight of Africa's peoples requires.

But, as we have seen, debt is not just a problem arising from external powers, and external debt remission will not resolve all Africa's problems. The key task which must accompany debt remission is internal political reform, reforms which dethrone sacralized politics, and which connect the Christian conception of politics as the quest for justice with plural arrangements of democratic government. As Bediako says:

> The major challenge now facing the Christian churches in the African political sphere is to raise to consciousness in the wider society the connection between the Church's message of righteousness, love and justice, and the search for sustainable democratic governance. (Bediako, 1995)

Sources

African Centre for Monetary Studies (1992), *Debt-Conversion Schemes in Africa: Lessons from the Experience of Developing Countries* (London: James Currey)

Elizabeth Amoah and Mercy Amba Oduyoye (1988), 'The Christ for African Women' in Virginia Fabella and Mercy Amba Oduyoye (eds.), *With Passion and Compassion: Third World Women Doing Theology* (Maryknoll, NY: Orbis Books)

Kwame Bediako (1982), 'Biblical Christologies in the Context of African Traditional Religions' in Vinay Samuel and Chris Sugden (eds.), *Sharing Jesus in the Two Thirds World* (Bangalore: Partnership in Mission-Asia)

Kwame Bediako (1995), *Christianity in Africa: The Renewal of a Non-Western Religion* (Edinburgh: Edinburgh University Press)

Fantu Cheru (1989), *The Silent Revolution in Africa: Debt, Development and Democracy* (London: Zed Books)

Katie Duckworth (1997), 'Two Births and a Funeral: Report on a Visit to Tanzania' (Mimeograph, Christian Aid)

Food and Agriculture Organization (1993), *Debt-for-Nature Swaps to Promote Natural Resource Conservation* (Rome: FAO)

Felipe Larrain and Andres Velasco (1990), *Can Swaps Solve the Debt Crisis? Lessons from the Chilean Experience* (Princeton, NJ: International Finance Section, Department of Economics, Princeton University)

John Mbiti (1972), 'Some African Concepts of Christology' in Georg F. Vicedom (ed.) *Christ and the Younger Churches* (London: SPCK)

John Mbiti (1973), 'HO SOTER EMON as an African Experience' in Barnabaas Lindars and Stephen S. Smalley (eds.), *Christ and Spirit in the New Testament* (Cambridge: Cambridge University Press)

Nioki Kote-Nikoi (1996), *Beyond the New Orthodoxy: Africa's Debt and Development Crisis in Retrospect* (Aldershot: Avebury)

Organization for Economic Cooperation and Development (1997), *Debt and Development Co-operation: Debt Relief Actions by DAC Members* (Paris: OECD)

John Parratt (1995), *Reinventing Christianity: African Theology Today* (Grand Rapids, MI: Eerdmans)

Jeffrey D. Sachs (1989), *New Approaches to the Latin American Debt Crisis* (Princeton, NJ: International Finance Section, Department of Economics, Princeton University)

Paul Spray (1997), *Change the DEBT Rules: A Basic Policy Paper* (London: Christian Aid)

Rainer Tetzlaff (1991), 'LLDCs (Least Developed Countries): The Fourth World in the Debt Trap' in Elmar Altvater, Kurt Hübner, Jochen Lorentzen and Raúl Rojas (eds.), transl. Terry Bond, *The Poverty of Nations: A Guide to the Debt Crisis – From Argentina to Zaire* (London: Zed Books)

Organizations

The following organizations are actively campaigning for urgent debt remission. Their websites contain much information on the campaign and on the range of actions which supporters can engage in:

Jubilee 2000 Coalition PO Box 100, London SE1 7RT
Tel: +44 (0)171 401 9999
Fax: +44 (0)171 401 3999
E-mail: mail@jubilee2000uk.org
Website: Jubilee 2000 http://www.jubilee2000uk.org/

Third World Network 228 Macalister Rd, 10400 Penang, Malaysia
Tel: 60 4 226 6728
Fax: 60 4 226 4505
E-mail: twn@igc.apc.org or twnpen@twn.po.my
Website: http://www.twnside.org.sg
Contact: Martin Khor

CAFOD Campaigns Office, Romero Close, Stockwell Rd, London SW9 9TY
Tel: 0171 733 7900
E-mail: hqcafod@cafod.org.ukCAFOD
Website: http://www.cafod.org.uk/shoe_action.htm

Christian Aid 35 Lower Marsh, Waterloo, London SE1 7RT
Tel: 0171 620 4444
Fax: 0171 620 0719
Website: http://www.christian-aid.org.uk/main.htm

European Network on Debt and Development
http://www.oneworld.org/eurodad/

The following organization is involved in health care in Tanzania:

Friends of Mvumi 24 Staverton Road, Oxford, OX2 6XJ
http://www.harefield.nthames.nhs.uk/mvumiweb/

5 Structurally Adjusted Poverty

The Generosity of a Mother of Twins in a Shanty Town in Addis Ababa

I live in a large shanty town on the eastern edge of Addis Ababa. If you were to come to our town you would see that in some ways we are blessed. Ethiopia is a mountainous country and we live high above the plain and the temperature is very good, not too hot, and you only need one blanket at night. Our houses are mostly made of mud. The ground is rough and stony but the houses are built in traditional style in groups around a square. We like to live in community and this means we can share what we have and keep an eye on each other's children. We cook for one another and this saves precious charcoal, and time. I often bake *injera*, the national food, which is like giant pancakes, and sell it to the other families as I have no other source of income and no husband to support me.

I am Hannah and I am twenty-five years old and have a daughter aged seven and twins who are one year old. My husband just ran off when the twins were born. He said he could not cope with three children. I have never seen him since. I was really desperate, I had to leave our small house where his casual labour paid the rent. I heard from friends about this tiny place which used to be a tobacco kiosk, which is why it is even smaller than the other houses. The room costs me 40 *birr* (£4) a month which I have to pay in advance. There is only room in here for a mattress and a stove, and the shelves on the back wall left from the tobacco selling where I keep my few pots and clothes. To get inside you have to crawl through a low door. In the daytime we let down a big shutter, where the tobacconist used to sell from, but when it is closed it is dark as there is no window.

Since my husband left I have no means of support and I think I would have died and my children too but I heard about an organization which helps families with twins. A lot of twins are born in Ethiopia. It is called the Gemini Trust. I went to their compound, which is a long bus ride from here into the city centre, with the twins and my older daughter and they talked to me and fed me and the children. They support us now as a family and even help to pay our rent. We go there every day. They give me the bus ticket and when we are there they feed the children and I get a meal as well. We get bread and a special (nutritional) biscuit. Since going there I have been able to feed the twins, who were very sick from hunger as my milk dried up before I went to Gemini. We still do not get any fruit or vegetables but we are not hungry like before.

In the nutritional centre I made friends with other mothers. We were sometimes twenty families in there, all with twins in a big room with mattresses, just feeding and talking. We were there for the whole day before getting back on the bus to come home, the children quiet and fed, and us with some food in our stomachs as well. We all became good friends and could share our difficulties. It was good to see other people getting better, just like me and my twins. One day one of my friends arrived in tears with her twins. Membrat told that her husband had beaten her and thrown her and the twins out of the house and she had wandered the street that night before coming to Gemini. She had no relatives she could go to and she did not know where she would sleep. I said she must come and stay with us. And so there are now two families in my tiny house. We just manage to fit on the mattress at night. It is a terrible squash and there is a lot of cleaning and carrying to do, but we help each other.

We get water by bucket from a standpipe a few hundred yards from the room but we have to pay for each bucket. We also buy charcoal and *teff*, the local grain, which is what I use to cook *injera*. We eat some of it and what we sell pays for the

water and fuel. I used to earn money cleaning people's houses.
Once I worked in a big house but then when the twins came
along I lost that job. It is hard keeping the children clean when
you have to pay for every bucket of water. It is also hard to
keep our clothes decent. People often pass on clothes for the
children to us when their children grow out of them. I wear the
dress that many Ethiopian women wear. It is off-white and long
(something like a sari) but it has to be washed a lot to keep
clean and when it wears out I find it very hard to buy another.
There used to be a second-hand clothes market in the city but
the government closed it down. They said it was taking money
away from local clothing workshops.

Ruth, my older daughter, is now seven and she goes to school.
I could not manage the cost but Gemini help us with this as
well. There are all kinds of new charges which have been
introduced for schooling. First there is a registration fee. Then
there is a parents' club fee and a sports club fee. We also have
to pay for books. Some schools even charge parents for the
desks. They do not have desks at Ruth's school, just timber
benches. She goes to school in the morning only. The classes
are very large – 120 children. And in the afternoon the school
takes in another batch of children. It is very overcrowded and
the teachers are not paid enough so they get other jobs to
supplement. But at least Ruth is going to school. Some of my
relatives in the rural area cannot send their children. They have
no money for the charges and in any case they need them to
tend their goats.

We are so grateful for Gemini. Without them we would not be
here today. But Gemini will only support us until the youngest
children are aged five. They will try to help us into some means
of making money before then. Some of the mothers do basket
weaving. They grow grass near their houses and they sell the
baskets through Gemini. Gemini also do other projects. They
have a project for street children. There are thousands of them
living on the city streets. They organized a dance and drama
acted by the street children which was called 'Adugna' and lots
of big people came to see it, government officials and

ambassadors. One of my friends went to see it in Mesal
Square where they performed one night in front of a big crowd.

Adjusting the Poor to the Demands of World Finance

The earliest known ancestor of the human race, called 'Din-
qenesh' (which means 'you are amazing') by Ethiopians, was
discovered in the Afar Desert in Ethiopia in 1974 (Haile-
Selassie, 1997). But the land which is the birthplace of humanity
became a byword for civil war, refugee-filled tent cities, and
epic famines in the 1970s and 1980s. The long-standing civil
war was the major cause of the cataclysm which overtook the
proud people of Ethiopia in those years. The socialist regime of
Mengistu also contributed to a dreadful record of endemic
poverty and negative development with its extreme centraliz-
ing policies, and in particular the collectivization of agriculture
and the nationalization of industrial production.

Relative political stability has returned to Ethiopia since 1991
when the Mengistu government finally collapsed. But the years
of feuding and famine, combined with over-centralized state
control, have taken a dreadful toll on land and people alike.
Ethiopia was left with considerable external debts, virtually no
industrial production capacity, and land as its only mobilizable
resource. But the land is worn out from too much farming.
While the countryside in many parts looks green and lush, and
climatic conditions are generally favourable, deforestation on
the hills has affected rainfall levels and reduced water reten-
tion, and led to widespread land erosion and the silting up of
rivers. More than a million tons of topsoil are washed into the
rivers every year (Parker, 1995).

There are 55 million people in Ethiopia on a land area more
than four times the size of the UK, but the proportion of fertile
land for farming is gradually going down. The population has
doubled in the last fifty years and will double again in the next
twenty-five if poverty and poor education are not addressed.
Parts of Ethiopia are already desert, other parts are in danger of
becoming desert. In response to the dangers of soil erosion, the
Ethiopian government has developed one of the largest tree-

planting schemes in the world. In the province of Tigray, 40 million tree seedlings were planted in one year alone. Hillsides are also being newly terraced with small stone walls, and old terracing is being repaired, to reduce erosion, and to provide more land for cultivation.

But these measures are a race against time. As one observer comments: 'The covenant between humankind and nature has been broken throughout Ethiopia. When nature has failed to provide, humans have failed to preserve' (Parker, 1995).

People in Ethiopia live on average for 48 years, as compared to 76 years in the UK or the USA. This low figure reflects the number of children and mothers who die in childbirth. Of 1,000 infants, 120 do not survive their first year and 200 out of 1,000 children do not survive until their fifth birthday. An Ethiopian consumes 1,600 calories of food in a typical day compared to the 3,200 calories consumed on average by a North American. This food intake is only 70 per cent of the minimum the body needs for good health. Less than one third of boys and one quarter of girls attend primary school, and half of them drop out before they reach the age of eleven. Less than half the men, and one third of the women, are active in the cash economy, and for those like Hannah who have no source of sustenance other than the cash economy it is a very poor provider.

After war-ravaged Mozambique, Ethiopia is the second poorest country in the world, and indebted to the extent of $5 billion to governments, institutions and banks in the North. Around half the debt is owed to the former USSR for arms purchased by the Mengistu regime for the civil war. Ethiopia's principal exports have been dramatically devalued in the last twenty years, partly because of the plummeting price of coffee which is the major export earner, and partly because of the World Bank and International Monetary Fund-imposed devaluation of the Ethiopian *birr*. This greatly reduced the amount of foreign exchange earned by exports, and increased the cost of essential imports such as fuel, machinery, spare parts and cooking oil.

Ethiopia is a country in need of complete reconstruction, much as Europe was after the Second World War. There are very few metalled roads in the country, and the dirt roads which do exist are ravaged by potholes and broken bridges. Only a quarter of the people have access to clean water. Electricity generation is sporadic and is only available in the largest urban settlements. Schools and hospitals are broken down and millions of private houses, offices and shops in the cities are in complete disrepair. Around a million people are still living in refugee camps, most of them refugees from continuing conflicts in Somalia and Sudan. Ethiopia also suffers from a chronic brain drain as educated young people leave the country in droves for jobs in the developed world (Cheru, 1994).

The new government has made sterling efforts towards a rehabilitation programme. Rural roads are being improved while better seeds and fertilizers are being made available to rural farmers. Private capital is being encouraged to provide and improve transport infrastructure and there is an increased reliance on markets in agricultural production which has had the intended effect of increasing rural food production (Hansson, 1995). But reconstruction on the scale that is needed is hampered by the burden of Ethiopia's $5 billion external debt. Most foreign exchange which comes into the country from exports goes straight out again to pay interest on the debt. In 1991, Ethiopia earned $139 million from the export of coffee and paid out $100 million in debt-interest payments (Parker, 1995). Although a small proportion of the debt was cancelled in 1992, the debt continues to grow as interest piles up.

Like all heavily indebted poor countries, Ethiopia's economy is run according to the requirements of the structural adjustment programme which the World Bank and the International Monetary Fund have imposed on Ethiopia as condition for new loans which allow it to meet interest and repayments on the old ones. As we have seen, the underlying economic assumptions of this programme are first that rolling back the state and economic liberalization will automatically produce economic growth and 'development' and, second, that capitalist economic development will bring about democracy (Konings, 1996).

However, the situation in Ethiopia, as in so many countries

subjected to adjustment, belies the simplicity of the adjustment prescription. In relation to rolling back the state, it is evident that without state-directed reconstruction and state support for small farmers and tree planting, Ethiopia would stand no chance of escaping from desperate poverty, or rescuing its shattered environment, for decades to come. And concerning political reform which deregulation is supposed to promote, democracy re-emerged in Ethiopia before adjustment had any effect. The post-Mengistu transitional government ruled for four years until 1995 when general elections were held. The transitional government set in train a process whereby the various regions of Ethiopia would be granted semi-autonomy, and Eritrea has already been granted full independence. Thus democratic reform has preceded economic reforms. There is now a growing concern that the severity of the economic reforms required by foreign bankers, far from promoting democracy, may actually drive Ethiopia back into civil war, as has happened in Rwanda and other parts of Africa. As Claude Ake comments:

> There is a contradiction between structural adjustment and democratization because of the specific forms that structural adjustment takes. In some cases the reduction in government expenditures by as much as 60 per cent is proposed. Can you imagine the reduction of government expenditures in the United States by as much as even 15 per cent and the effects?
>
> Of course, the result of this is that social consensus is breaking down all over the continent. The degree of political coercion, authoritarianism and the degree of violence that is used to impose these kinds of policies is creating very new and complex problems for Africa. (Ake, 1992)

The basic thesis of the Western economists who control the budgets of indebted African countries is that the market is the key promoter of development and democracy, whereas the state is a hindrance to both. They argue that this thesis is borne out by the fact that so much of Africa's debt has been unwisely spent on prestige projects and the military by governments out of touch with their people. But African economists believe that this thesis is deeply flawed and that its proponents have failed to take account of a number of factors that are unique to the African context.

First, Africa suffers from a unique and excessive dependence on world commodity markets because so much of the African economy is still reliant on exports of primary commodities to earn foreign exchange to buy essential imported goods which it still does not have the capacity to produce for itself. This translates into a fundamental structural weakness which was particularly exposed in the worldwide recession of the 1980s. It also leaves Africa particularly vulnerable to new so-called 'free-trade' regimes which incorporate significant elements of tariff production for manufactured goods and markets in the North while barring similar protection for goods and markets in the South.

Second, Africa's is a deeply fragmented economy comprised of more than fifty nations with no effective continental and internal trading market analogous to those of Europe, the Americas or East Asia. And third, Africa suffers from a deep identity crisis of which the brain drain is just one, though a significant, symptom. Despite the fact that Africa has had such an influence on Western culture and history for more than two hundred years, educated Africans come to view their continent and culture through Western eyes. This undermines their confidence in their own cultural perspectives and riches, and, as Adebayo Adedeji says, makes them 'vulnerable to manipulation by whichever structure that apparently wields power, be it an international development agency, a developed country or another more conscientious developing country' (Adedeji, 1992).

Adebayo Adedeji is the former Executive Secretary of the UN Economic Commission for Africa. For some time the Commission has proposed an alternative African approach to economic and political adjustment, rather than the programme of reforms imposed on Africa by the Washington-based institutions of the World Bank and the International Monetary

Fund. The Commission advocates adjustment which is human-centred, noting that structural adjustment in the 1980s produced at best ambiguous results even when evaluated on purely economic criteria. African countries which resisted the reforming zeal of the Bank sustained higher levels of internal production, earned more from exports, and imported less than countries which embraced, mostly under extreme duress, the structural adjustment medicine.

The Commission also found that World Bank efforts to present structural adjustment as a success relied on dubious or even anomalous statistics, and on special pleading that reforming countries had only performed worse than non-reformers because they faced worse conditions in their particular export markets (Mihevc, 1993).

One of the central aims of structural adjustment is purportedly a shift of resources from urban to rural areas. This is supposed to be realized by reductions in state intervention in markets for food which primarily benefit non-farming city dwellers, and state investment in industry and public service provision which again is greatest in cities. However, the abolition or reform of government food-marketing agencies often did not produce the increases in prices received by farmers for food products which the Bank suggested they would. They did though raise the price of basic foodstuffs for the urban poor, and for those rural poor who are unable to produce enough food to feed themselves. Similarly, reforms designed to shift available local investment funds from urban-based industries and public services such as education towards rural production of export crops simply resulted in massively increased urban and rural unemployment, while at the same time contributing to world surpluses in the export crops, which lowered world prices and reduced their value.

Many critics of structural adjustment have also pointed out the particularly dire impact of adjustment on women. Women in all African cultures bear the primary responsibility for child-rearing, for housekeeping, water-carrying, cooking, and often for food-growing as well. Women in urban areas like Hannah are therefore doubly victims of structural adjustment, first because structural adjustment has reduced the availability of employment in cities, and second because structural adjustment has increased the cost of food and child-rearing (Elson, 1989). In rural areas, while crop prices paid to farmers may have gone up because of the abolition of price controls, women peasant farmers may still not be able to take advantage of this because growing more crops takes more time which is time away from other essential family tasks. Furthermore, women agricultural labourers are adversely affected by increased crop prices as they have to pay more for their food while their pay does not increase (Elson, 1989).

Structural adjustment in essence is an economic theory which suggests that money and markets, when given free rein, are the best managers of natural and human resources. Only the market is said to be capable of distributing resources such that the poor can find food at prices they can afford and work at adequate levels of remuneration. This theory rests on the fundamental assumption that the state is inherently a worse manager of a nation's resources than are liberalized markets. This assumption is held so tenaciously by most modern Western 'neoclassical' economists that all evidence to the contrary is ignored, or explained away as a consequence of market imperfections. The evidence that poverty in Africa is rising in both urban and rural areas, or that countries which have not undergone adjustment have less poverty and stronger economies, is discounted because it contradicts fundamental articles of faith in the current rebirth of classical economic theory which only a global depression on the scale of the 1930s would seem to have any chance of shifting.

In response to criticism that adjustment exacerbates poverty, the World Bank has argued that adjustment and poverty eradication are really two sides of the same coin and that without adjustment poverty in Africa would be worse than it is. The Bank maintains that economic growth is the only means to help the poor and that more growth can only come from pursuing structural adjustment more rigorously (World Bank, 1990b). The more the market is given free rein, the better the poor will be able to increase their production at prices which justly remunerate them. They will be able to do this by maximizing their 'comparative advantage' of low-wage and labour-intensive production, advantages which are particularly relevant to primary commodity production.

The Bank has begun to admit that adjustment may hit the poor and they have come up with some measures to counter this. They propose that education cuts should be targeted on universities and not on primary schools and that cuts in health care provision, and health care charges, should be focused more on urban than rural areas. They also commend targeted help for those adversely affected by adjustment such as retraining for workers laid off in public spending cuts and privatization schemes, and credit schemes in rural areas.

However, the Bank continues to take the view that state-targeted poverty eradication programmes will undermine the adjustment and liberalization programme. Adjustment itself will ultimately deliver poverty eradication provided it is embraced consistently and in the long term. In the short term the poor need to be remobilized economically and re-educated about their needs. One suggestion is that 'the poor can sometimes reduce the value of their consumption without adverse nutritional effects by switching from superior food to inferior foods that are less costly (but as nutritious)' (World Bank, 1990a). As John Mihevc notes, such Bank statements reveal a disturbingly paternalistic and simplistic approach to poverty (Mihevc, 1993). They also demonstrate the gap between the Bank's rhetoric about poverty, and the tenacity of its long-standing commitment to market reforms and growth, regardless of the victims.

As one of the Bank's earlier critics, Robert Ayres, notes, despite much talk about poverty eradication, and the diversion of a small proportion of its funds towards poverty eradication schemes, the primary objective of the Bank's operation is to serve 'the economic and political interests of American foreign policy' (Ayres, 1983). In the 1960s and 1970s these interests were aligned with resistance to the influence of the Soviet bloc in Africa. Aid and lending, and especially military lending, to African regimes was predicated on their stance in the East-West

Cold War, and not on their record in respecting human rights, eradicating poverty or promoting democracy. In the 1990s the flow of new money to Africa from America was much reduced, reflecting the end of the Cold War, and a reduced US strategic interest in the region.

Most new loans which are directed toward Africa are paid by the World Bank and the International Monetary Fund to earlier lenders and creditors of African governments, and increasingly by the World Bank to itself as lender of last resort. The consequent increased flow of resources out of Africa towards the USA (and Europe), whether of reduced price natural commodities or of foreign exchange, therefore reflects the new strategic interest of Washington which is ultimately determined by the USA's desire to maintain a very high standard of living for its own people despite unprecedented levels of government debt, and a large balance-of-payments deficit to the rest of the world.

The hypocrisy and double standards of structural adjustment policies, and their ineffectiveness in promoting real democratic development, are both highlighted in a significant speech made by the Vice-President of the World Bank, Joseph Stiglitz, in Helsinki, Finland, in January 1998. He describes the policies which underlie what he calls the Washington Consensus as 'misguided' because they neglect fundamental development issues, are 'sometimes even misleading', and fail to address 'vital questions' (Stiglitz, 1998). He notes that if the package of policies imposed on debtor countries had been followed in the United States 'the remarkable expansion of the US economy ... would have been thwarted'. And he points out that whereas Russia followed the Washington Consensus line, China did not, and as a consequence 'real incomes and consumption have fallen in the former Soviet empire, and real incomes and consumption have risen remarkably rapidly in China' (Stiglitz, 1998).

Stiglitz argues that a crucial reason for the failure of the Washington Consensus is that the economic package it promotes is narrowly designed to achieve increases in measured GDP, whereas 'we seek increases in living standards –

including improved health and education. We seek equitable development which ensures that all groups in society enjoy the fruits of development, not just the few at the top. And we seek democratic development' (Stiglitz, 1998).

In the rest of his speech Stiglitz knocks down all of the key pillars of structural adjustment programmes. He notes that moderate inflation, below 40 per cent, is neither harmful nor costly. He points out that public spending budget deficits, provided they are used for such key development areas as education, health and physical infrastructure, produce very high returns on investment and are therefore justified. He argues that monetary stability, the principal goal of structural adjustment programmes, is a poor guide to genuine economic stability, and that reductions in unemployment are a much better way of achieving economic (and social) stability, even when pump-primed by public spending. He also notes that the benefits of privatization have been wildly overestimated by its advocates while its costs have been underestimated. The crucial issue is not ownership but competition and private monopolies are no better, and may be worse, than public ones:

> The unspoken premise [of the Washington Consensus] is that governments are presumed to be worse than markets ... I do not believe [that] ... left to itself, the market will tend to underprovide human capital ... Without government action there will be too little investment in the production and adoption of new technology. (Stiglitz, 1998)

In sum, Stiglitz contends, 'the dogma of liberalization has become an end in itself and not a means to a better financial system'. And this misguided dogma is applied to indebted nation states undergoing enforced adjustment by economists representing the Washington Consensus who only examine simple accounting data and then 'fly into a country, look at and attempt to verify these data, and make macroeconomic recommendations for policy reforms, all in the space of a couple of weeks' (Stiglitz, 1998). Stiglitz calls for an alternative approach to development and to the problems of indebted poor countries which does not assume that Washington economists have all the answers, and which is much more humble in approaching the problems of debtor nations.

The United Nations Economic Commission for Africa has for a long time been challenging what Stiglitz calls the Washington Consensus and proposing an African alternative adjustment programme. The basic aim of this programme is to make African countries self-reliant (a self-reliance which as we have seen is still the driving force behind agricultural subsidies and tariffs in Europe and North America). The first priority in the quest for self-reliance is self-sufficiency in food (Adedeji, 1992). Hannah is among half a billion Africans who depend on imported food. To achieve self-sufficiency more needs to be done to support small subsistence farmers and to improve their farming practices, instead of the current tendency to move former subsistence farms into the production of cash crops for export.

In pursuing this objective of self-reliance the Commission contends that African governments should act together and be more strident in persuading the West of the urgent need for a debt plan involving radical debt relief which is not tied to the usual package of rescheduling and economic stringencies of the Bank and the International Monetary Fund. Without debt repayment, and the forced export of primary commodities for foreign exchange for debt servicing, even the poorest African countries would be able to feed their own people and would not need demeaning food aid. Without debt servicing they would also not be dependent on Western aid projects and funds to resource sanitation, clean water and health care programmes (ECA, 1989). In Ghana, for example, for every $4 which is currently spent on health care, $27 is exported for debt servicing.

The Commission also propose that wealth in Africa needs to be more equitably distributed and utilized. Taxes on capital and on the rich need to be more consistently imposed, and collected, and new tax revenues used for social needs provision, including specific policies to make essential foodstuffs and other basic needs items available to the poor. At the same time military spending should be reduced while public investment in key infrastructural projects such as roads, bridges, hospitals and schools is increased (ECA, 1989). The other key element in the alternative adjustment programme is the building up of the internal African economy such that inter-African trade grows in significance. This approach to interstate trade has realized considerable benefits to developing nations in East Asia and would help African nations to enhance their economic power relative to other strong trading blocs such as the European Union and the new North American Free Trade Area.

Advocates of an African alternative to the Washington Consensus on adjustment also point out that adjustment as conceived in Washington is always one way and that this one-way adjustment fails to take account of the wealth and natural resources which have been drained from Africa in more than two hundred years of colonial and post-colonial exploitation. Moreover, the conditions imposed on African states under structural adjustment have meant that key ministries in many African governments are effectively being run by economists and officials from the World Bank and the International Monetary Fund. This direct foreign control of African governments represents in effect a resumption of colonial control, and exploitation, in a new guise (Mkandawire, 1994).

Ethiopia Will Stretch Out Her Hands to God

More than half of the population of Ethiopia are members of the Ethiopian Orthodox Church. Ethiopians are a very religious people and their favourite Bible quotation from Psalm 68.31, 'Ethiopia will stretch out her hands to God', is often used as a motto or in heraldic symbols. Christianity came to Ethiopia in 341 AD when two young Christian men from Tyre, Frumentius and Aedesius, were shipwrecked in the Red Sea, off the Ethiopian coast, and were rescued and brought to the court of Ethiopia at Axum where they introduced the royal court to the Christian faith, whence it spread among the people. Frumentius was later consecrated as bishop by the North African Bishop of Alexandria, St Athanasius.

Missionaries from Syria and Egypt continued to aid the

Christian conversion of Ethiopia and by 500 AD the Ethiopian Orthodox Church had become the dominant religious institution in Ethiopia, and remains so to this day in a region of Africa which is predominantly and strongly Muslim. For more than a thousand years the Ethiopian Orthodox Church was led by Coptic monks from Egypt, reflecting its early missionary origins. But in the 1920s the Emperor Haile Selassie pressed for greater independence and, after the Italian occupation of Ethiopia during the Second World War, the Ethiopian Church finally achieved full autonomy from its mother church in Egypt.

Orthodox church ceremonies play a central role in the life of many Ethiopians, as they do in much of the Eastern Orthodox world. Orthodox Christianity is a religion which embraces the whole of life. Its Scriptures, liturgies, priests and rituals form a religious culture which is inherently conservative of ancient traditions, and resistant to the winds of cultural change from the West, though by no means impervious.

The cornerstone of Orthodox theology is the doctrine of the incarnation which understands Jesus Christ as a fully human being who is also God in human form. St Athanasius, the fourth-century Bishop of Alexandria, and one of the foremost theologians in the Eastern tradition, argued that by drawing the full experience of human life into divine life, Christ transformed fallen human nature into the eternal, divine life of the sacred Trinity: 'God was made man that we might become gods'. Orthodox Christians understand that this transformation of human life into a sharing in the life of God becomes a reality for Christian believers through their sharing and participation in the sacramental and liturgical life of the church which carries forward on earth the transformative power of the incarnate and risen Christ after his ascension, and before his coming again (Ware, 1979).

The second coming of Jesus also plays a central role in Orthodox theology and liturgy. Unlike most moderns, the Orthodox do not believe that civilization is on an upward path from darkness to light and that the human condition is on an upward path as history progresses. On the contrary, their theology leads them to expect suffering and calamities and they believe, as did the earliest Christians, that after a period of time when these sufferings have become particularly intense, the Antichrist will appear. The Antichrist will be a human being who for a brief time will exercise an evil global authority over all the peoples of the world. His evil reign will come to an end with the return of Jesus Christ to judge the world. For many Orthodox recent history seems to point to the coming of the Antichrist as they have been subjected to great persecution in Turkey, Albania, Georgia, Lebanon and Israel, while in Ethiopia famine and war have worn down the churches, their clergy and people.

The theology of incarnation, together with a profound belief in the bodily resurrection of Jesus Christ from the dead, are both of central importance to this future or eschatological orientation of the Orthodox. They believe that at the last judgement, which is said to bring the current phase of fallen human history to its end, the earth and the people and creatures of the world will be renewed to their full and pristine physical glory, as before the fall. As the second-century Eastern theologian St Irenaeus said:

> Neither the structure nor the substance of creation is destroyed. It is only the 'outward form of this world' (1 Cor. 7.31) that passes away – that is to say, the conditions produced by the fall. And when this 'outward form' has passed away, man will be renewed and will flourish in a prime of life that is incorruptible, so that it is no longer possible for him to grow old any more. There will be a 'new heaven and a new earth' (Rev. 21.1); and in this new heaven and new earth man shall abide, for ever new and for ever conversing with God. (Ware, 1979)

There is then a strong physicality to Orthodox hope in the future. In the present this is evident in a whole array of physical and visible forms of the presence of salvation, and of future hope, in the life and worship of the church and her people, and also in development projects sponsored by the Ethiopian Orthodox Church. Holy Communion is considered the central liturgical act and is seen as an objective physical event which is also a very joyful occasion as believers are changed when they receive the divine life within them.

This sense for the sacramental character of human existence, when lived and experienced in the light of the redeeming incarnation of Jesus Christ, is not limited to the traditional sacraments of Eucharist and baptism. All of life for the Ethiopian Orthodox has a sacramental quality. The icons that adorn Orthodox churches and monasteries are windows on to the divine to guide the physical senses towards the vision of God. So too are the frequent fasts through which the devout of the Ethiopian Orthodox regulate times and seasons, and the practices of food-growing, child-rearing and home-building of their daily lives.

The liturgies of the incarnation (Timkat), Epiphany, the Passion and Easter, form the central events in the Ethiopian Orthodox year. At Timkat the sacred tabot – a tablet of wood or stone which represents the ark of the covenant and is kept in the inner sanctuary of the church into which only the priests may enter – is brought out of the church and held overhead throughout the night by the priests who wear spectacular and colourful clothes. The wondrous chants and beautiful physical symbolism of the Orthodox liturgy are reminders of the supreme and transcendent holiness of God. They also link worshippers on earth and in the present to the eternal life of the divine, which God shares with humanity through the incarnation. This dual sense of the transcendence and the immanence of God is powerfully communicated in the following prayer from the Ethiopian Orthodox liturgy:

> God is the most high, to whom none can attain, but he
> became humble among us.
> God is the untouchable fire:
> but we saw him and felt him,
> and ate and drank with him
> *Liturgy of the Ethiopian Orthodox Church*

The Holy God brings salvation to humanity by allowing humans to share in the divine life of the Holy Trinity. Christ shares to the full in our weakness and poverty and this sharing of divine life with the human is the precondition for the transformation of our poverty and sinfulness into eternal life.

Orthodox theologians such as Philip Sherrard argue that it is because the West has lost touch with this deeply incarnational theology of the God who is also human that Western culture and institutions have had such a devastating impact on the peoples and environments of the non-Western world. In contrast to the sacramental and spiritual meaning of our humanness as revealed and redeemed in the God-Man Jesus Christ, the Western secular view of persons, and especially the reduction of persons to producers and consumers in modern economics, obscures the divine essence and potential of human being and becoming:

> Modern man's chief heresy about himself consists in the fact that he thinks he is or can be man without any inner dynamic relationship with God, without that reciprocity and inter-penetration of the divine and the human of which the model is the Incarnate Logos. Having rejected the understanding that his life and activity are significant only in so far as they incarnate, reflect and radiate that transcendent spiritual reality which is the ground and centre of his own being, he is condemned to believe that he is the autocratic and omnipotent ruler of his own affairs, and of the world about him, which it is his duty to subdue, organize, investigate and exploit to serve his profane mental curiosity or his acquisitive material appetites. (Sherrard, 1987)

The paradox is that just when modern humans believe themselves to be most in control of their destiny, and the destiny of the earth, through the instruments of technological control, markets, and consumer choice, they find that they are most in subjection to global forces and structures, such as global financial markets and global corporations, over which they have less and less control.

In affluent societies in the North this growing loss of control over daily life creates stress and unease, and results in the insecurities of unemployment or of temporary contracts both at work and even in the family. In the South, as we have seen, these same global forces and structures are even more destructive. The enslavement of whole societies to the dehumanizing, but humanly generated, forces of globalization is an extreme example of the cruelty and misery which issue from the denial of the spiritual origin and orientation of our humanness. The enslavement of human life to the authority of money is a manifestation of what Sherrard sees as the modern deification of (fallen) humanity, and the consequent denial of the transcendent ground of the true meaning of personhood as revealed in the incarnation:

> The deification of man as a fallen mortal entity has led, as we are only too well aware, to the most extreme forms of cruelty and rapacity, forms which deny the unique and absolute value of the human person and of every other created reality. The assertion that man is merely human has resulted in a dehumanization possibly without parallel in the history of the world. (Sherrard, 1987)

In Orthodox perspective the only guarantor of the true spiritual worth of persons is Christian humanism, a spiritual humanism which issues from the recognition of the universal significance of the incarnation of Jesus Christ, in whom the eternal and spiritual meaning of humanness was revealed in history, redeemed through relationship with divinity.

The loss of the spiritual meaning of personhood in secular cultures is directly linked to the endless quest for material fulfilment through consumerism which is dominant in most affluent societies in the North, and which is doing so much damage both to the planet and to its peoples. Similarly, the distorted vision of the human future, represented by advocates of the 'Washington Consensus' and the global free market, is a debasement of the Christian hope of human, social and cosmic transformation as prefigured in the resurrection of Christ, and in the earnest expectation of Christ's second coming.

Like so many other utopian projects in the name of which political leaders have required costly human sacrifices, the putative utopia of the global market has created more victims than beneficiaries (Gray, 1998). In Orthodox perspective the only true utopia is the remaking of the world promised after the second coming of Christ. War, famine, and premature death are the all-too-frequent consequences of those eras in history when humans have invested their longing for redemption in this-worldly utopias, which require dreadful human sacrifices and ignore the potential for evil and sin as well as for good in such utopian visions. The eschewal of utopia here on earth does not of course mean that Christians, Orthodox or otherwise, are not engaged in a search for a more just and caring society here on earth. It does mean that Christians should acquire a habit of suspicion towards panaceas for all human ills proffered by secular economists, bankers or politicians.

In recognition of the spiritual meaning of personhood, Christians since the time of Jesus Christ have invested considerable efforts in alms-giving, in famine relief, and in healing the sick. They have also supported social arrangements that limit wealth and prevent the virtual enslavement of one group of people by another. Only since the invention of the global market (whose origins may be traced to the twelfth century), and the emergence of the Church (the Holy Roman Empire) as an imperialistic institution, has the Church become associated with imperial practices such as slavery, and the colonial subjugation of peoples, lands and natural resources to the economic interests of imperial powers with whom the churches both before and after the Reformation were frequently in inextricable partnership.

In the modern as in the ancient world the churches remain international communions, both in East and West. But the international form of their communion is increasingly detached from the political and economic interests of European or American imperialism. This means that the churches have a new potential to represent in global form the Christian insight into the spiritual meaning of humanness, and the divine origins of personhood and the natural order. As global institutions such as the International Monetary Fund, the World Bank and the World Trade Organization acquire unprecedented power over the welfare of billions of people, through the economic control which they exercise over indebted poor (but not indebted rich) countries, so global Christian churches and networks of churches such as the World Council of Churches have corresponding duties to exercise global pressure on such agencies, and to advance a view of humanness which can prevent the sacrifice of the lives of the poor to the utopian ideology of the free market.

Orthodox Christians, along with Protestant Christians, have used the fora of the World Council of Churches as one of the principal means for addressing global injustice. At its fiftieth anniversary meeting in Harare, Zimbabwe in December 1998, the World Council adopted the Jubilee 2000 call for debt forgiveness for unpayable debt for the poor countries of the world. In like manner, the Catholic Church, under both its present and previous Popes, has produced a consistent body of social and moral teaching on economic and political systems which has emphasized the priority of respect for persons and for human life over the tendencies of human industrial, technological and economic systems to subsume human welfare to the authority of money, or mammon. Pope John Paul II has also added his voice to those church leaders who are calling for debt forgiveness for poor countries in the South (John Paul II, 1995).

However, Christians cannot leave the struggle for debt forgiveness, and for justice in the global economy, to their leaders or global communions. The confession of the spiritual value of humanness also requires practical actions of love towards the neighbour. And in a globalized economic order every Christian, North and South, East and West, consequently has a duty to those who are becoming their neighbours in this new order. This means that decisions about what we buy, what we eat, and what we do with our money must go hand in hand with our worship of Jesus Christ and our prayers for the peace of the world.

One form of this duty is Christian giving to agencies such as Christian Aid which, in Ethiopia, as elsewhere in the world, work with churches and non-governmental agencies like the Gemini Trust in development projects which are designed to restore dignity, control and autonomy to local communities and regions. Christian Aid also supports the Development and Inter-Church Aid Commission of the Ethiopian Orthodox Church. Amongst various projects, DICAC is working in the villages north of Addis Ababa on what it calls 'spot spring developments'. The aim of this project is to give villagers better access to clean water, and water for irrigation, through improving the use and cleanliness of local water sources, which are most commonly springs.

Traditionally, communities which get water from open springs will also water their animals and wash their clothes in the water pool that gathers around the spring, thus risking contamination of the supply. The village priests are the ones who first advance the idea of the project. If the village elders back it, the materials and a project worker are brought in to resource the project. Each village only embarks on the project once all the people of the village have given it their full support and offered to participate in the water works. The project involves the local people identifying the best and most reliable water source. Using their own labour, local resources such as stone and sand, and technical materials provided by DICAC – such as bags of cement and plastic pipes and taps – the community enclose the spring and pipe the water to a closed storage tank fitted with collection taps and an overflow pipe running to an animal-watering trough. Where springs are distant from villages, pipes are laid in shallow trenches so the water storage can be located in the village. Where there are no springs, wells are dug which are then capped with concrete and fitted with handpumps. The project is simple and relies on the skills and resources of local people. In giving them more control over their own water resources it also teaches them basic community health principles around clean water, and the careful disposal of human and animal waste. The project also helps to establish local democracy as village councils are created to oversee the project and to ensure the subsequent maintenance of the upgraded water supply.

Spot spring development is just one small example of the enormous developmental potential of the culture of the village in improving the quality of life and access to natural resources of the predominantly rural peoples of Africa. It is also a good example of a self-reliant approach to development which values the resources and skills of local communities above monetary measures of economic development. It also expresses the principle of reciprocity between local people and development projects and goals which is central to a more holistic, and less economistic, understanding of human development.

The goals of the project are developed and shared with local people through their cultural agents, the priests, and the goals are realized primarily through the agency of the people themselves. Their ownership of the project is both an opportunity for education about their own potential to enhance their own welfare, and also a means to ensure the long-term viability of the project once the external partnership is withdrawn. The external partner acts as catalyser of the development potential of the local community rather than as agent working on its behalf, or in its name.

This kind of reciprocity in development interacts in significant ways with the Orthodox view of humanness. As we have seen, Orthodox worship and theology express a deep reciprocity between the divine and human natures of Christ, and between the redeeming power of the incarnation and the struggle for material security and welfare of daily human life. This affirmation of the reciprocity between the spiritual and material nature of human being provides a fertile conceptual base for a holistic and Christian vision of development that expresses respect for persons and for the material wealth which the natural world provides.

It also offers a theological ground for criticism of patterns of human development which prioritize economic measures above more holistic measures of human well-being, which include spiritual and relational as well as material dimensions. This approach is suggestive of a new model of human development in opposition to the economistic model imposed on countries throughout sub-Saharan Africa and elsewhere under the auspices of structural adjustment programmes. In the next chapter we will explore an alternative and more people-centred

model of development in more detail, looking also at its
traditional and spiritual roots.

Sources

Adebayo Adedeji (1992), 'The Dimensions of the Crisis' in David
Kennett and Tukumbi Lumumba-Kasongo (eds.), *Structural
Adjustment and the Crisis in Africa: Economic and Political Perspectives*
(Lewiston, NY: Edwin Mellen Press)

Claud Ake (1992), 'The Legitimacy Crisis of the State' in David
Kennett and Tukumbi Lumumba-Kasongo (eds.), *Structural
Adjustment and the Crisis in Africa: Economic and Political Perspectives*
(Lewiston, NY: Edwin Mellen Press, 1992)

Robert L. Ayres (1983), *Banking on the Poor: The World Bank and World
Poverty* (Cambridge, MA: MIT Press)

Fantu Cheru (1994), 'Designing a Structural Adjustment Programme:
Reconstruction, Rehabilitation and Long-Term Transformation' in
Abebe Zegeye and Siegfried Paesewang (eds.), *Ethiopia in Change:
Peasantry, Nationalism and Democracy* (London: British Academic
Press)

Economic Commission for Africa (1989), *African Alternative Framework
to Structural Adjustment Programmes for Socio-Economic Recovery and
Transformation* (Addis Ababa: ECA)

Diane Elson (1989), 'The Impact of Structural Adjustment on Women:
Concepts and Issues' in Bade Onimode (ed.), *The International
Monetary Fund, the World Bank and the African Debt, Volume 2: The
Social and Political Impact* (London: Zed Books)

John Gray (1998), *False Dawn: The Delusions of Global Capitalism*
(London: Granta)

Teferra Haile-Selassie (1997), *The Ethiopian Revolution 1974–1991: From
a Monarchical Autocracy to a Military Oligarchy* (London: Kegan Paul
International)

Göte Hansson (1995), *The Ethiopian Economy 1974–94: Ethiopia Tikdem
and After* (London: Routledge)

John Paul II (1995), *Tertio Millennio Adveniente* (London: Catholic
Truth Society)

Piet Konings (1996), 'The Post-Colonial State and Economic and
Political Reforms in Cameroon' in Alex E. Fernández Jilberto and
André Mommen (eds.), *Liberalization in the Developing World:
Institutional and Economic Changes in Latin America, Africa and Asia*
(London: Routledge)

Liturgy of the Ethiopian Orthodox Church (Eng. trans. Egyptian Book

Press, 1953) as reproduced in Janet Morley and Rebecca Dudley (1998), *Live In Hope: Order of Service for Christian Aid Week 1998* (London: Christian Aid)

John Mihevc (1993), *The Market Tells Them So: The World Bank and Economic Fundamentalism in Africa* (London: Zed Books)

Thandika Mkandawire (1994), 'Adjustment, Political Conditionality and Democratisation in Africa' in Giovanni Andrea Cornia and Gerald K. Helleiner (eds.), *From Adjustment to Development in Africa: Conflict, Controversy, Convergence, Consensus?* (London: St Martin's Press)

Ben Parker (1995), *Ethiopia: Breaking New Ground* (Oxford: Oxfam)

Philip Sherrard (1987), *The Rape of Man and Nature* (Ipswich: Golgonooza Press)

Joseph Stiglitz (1998), 'World economist re-evalutes economic dogma', *Huvustadbladet* (January) (Helsinki: Finland). Also at http://www.wider.unu.edu/tra9803.htm.

Kallistos Ware (1979), *The Orthodox Way* (London: Mowbrays)

World Bank (1990a), *Making Adjustment Work for the Poor in Africa* (Washington: World Bank)

World Bank (1990b), *World Development Report* (Washington: World Bank)

Organizations

Christian Aid 35 Lower Marsh, Waterloo, London, SE1 7RT
Telephone: 0171 620 4444
Fax: 0171 620 0719
http://www.christian-aid.org.uk/main.htm

Ethiopiad RCC 2063, Northampton, NN3 6BR

Oxfam 274 Banbury Road, Oxford, OX2 7DZ
http://www.oneworld.org/oxfam/

6 Finance for the Poor in Bangladesh

The Poor Furniture-Maker and the Professor of Economics

When Muhammad Yunus first met Sophia Khatoon she was only twenty-two years old but looked twice her age. Sophia was a furniture-maker living and working in the tiny village of Jobra in the south of Bangladesh just a few miles from Chittagong University where Yunus was working as a professor of economics. Sophia worked all day with bamboo, or ratan, soaking and steaming the material to make it pliable, shaping it into the arms, legs and supports for the stools and chairs she made, tacking and binding her creations together first with nails and then with thin strips of dried cane tightly woven. She made beautiful seats for her furniture with cross-weave cane and then varnished them before setting them out to dry. She was a skilled and efficient worker; she worked seven days a week, and from twelve to fourteen hours a day, and yet she lived in abject poverty. All the furniture she made she had to sell to a moneylender who provided the credit to buy the raw materials. The price she received barely covered the costs of the materials and was hardly enough to keep hunger at bay.

Professor Yunus calculated that Sophia was in effect paying interest to the moneylender on her line of credit for the purchase of bamboo and cane at the rate of 10 per cent a day, or more than 3,000 per cent a year. He found it astonishing that a woman with such skill who worked so hard, produced such beautiful bamboo furniture and created wealth at such a high rate was earning so little. He decided to lend Sophia the sum of 50 *tika*, equivalent to $5. With this small loan she was able to buy raw materials for herself, pay off the moneylender, and establish herself in self-employment. Within six months she increased her income sevenfold, and was able to repay the small loan which had enabled her to escape the abject poverty in which she had been living.

The meeting between Sophia and Yunus took place in the context of an action research project which Yunus had launched with his students in the late 1970s. He had returned from studying economics in the West and observed that after the famine of 1974 poverty in Bangladesh was getting worse not better. He saw that the traditional economic and development approaches which he was teaching in the university were failing to lift people out of poverty in Bangladesh where 70 per cent of the population are still classified as very poor. He decided that he and his students would go and talk to poor villagers like Sophia and ask them what it was that was keeping them poor, and what would make a difference. What they found was that the poor were not poor through lack of knowledge or skill but rather because of landlessness, and lack of availability of credit. Landlessness has been increasing in rural Bangladesh as in many other parts of South Asia, partly because of the impact of the 'green revolution' which required new and expensive agricultural inputs which have driven many small peasant farmers into debt so that they lose their land. Once they become landless, peasants are forced into the cash economy and it is then that they become subject to inhuman exploitation by employers, landowners and moneylenders. Peasants seeking self-employment have no option but to resort to moneylenders as a way out of the virtual slavery of low-wage agriculture because they are excluded from effective channels of credit and technical help. Banks will not lend to them because they have no collateral and thus they are kept in a cycle of debt, exploitation and poverty.

As a result of his findings Professor Yunus began to experiment with small-scale credit in one region in the south of Bangladesh, persuading a commercial bank to make small loans on collateral which he himself provided. Provided the loan period was kept fairly short and payments were made frequently – he started with daily payments and moved to weekly – Yunus found that the poor were very good at repaying their loans. Out of these early experiments in small loans to the poor was born the Grameen Bank which is now the largest microcredit organization in the world with $108 million under the control of its owner-members.

Yunus designed the Bank from the outset as one which would be run and owned by its members, the poor. Everyone who borrows from the bank is also encouraged to save 1 *taka* (3 cents) a week and once their saving reaches 100 *taka* they are able to buy one share in the Bank, which is all they need to become a shareholder as well as a borrower. The shareholder-borrowers elect nine of their number as directors of the Bank, while three are appointed by the Bangladeshi government which has supported the Bank in various ways.

The Bank's operations are a form of 'barefoot banking'. The fundamental principle on which the Bank works is that the poor have the capacity to help themselves out of poverty by their own efforts and skills, once freed from the cycle of indebtedness, low wages and high interest payments. They do not lack ideas, motivation or skill, nor do they need to change their attitudes to get out of poverty. It is the exploitative economic system, and the individuals who benefit from this system, which keeps them mired in poverty. Once they can get access to capital they can create their own wealth using their own natural talents, and the natural resources around them. The amount of capital they need is not great. A typical loan is between $60 and $70, on which interest at 20 per cent is charged to cover for inflation and the costs of the Bank, with a payback time of one year. The Bank finds that it takes the really destitute poor about ten such loans (and up to ten years) to escape from poverty into secure self-employment and a standard of living that adequately meets basic needs.

The Bank deploys 7,000 field workers who organize banking services in the 36,000 villages where its 2.1 million borrowers reside. The Bank has 1,100 branches and the field operations are focused on establishing groups of five borrowers who meet weekly and learn the Bank's rules and regulations and commit themselves to the 'Sixteen Decisions'. The Decisions are designed to raise social awareness and improve social practices among the members and were agreed at a national workshop of one hundred women centre-chiefs in 1984. The Decisions commit the members to the four basic principles of the Grameen Bank – discipline, unity, courage and hard work. The Decisions commit the members to the following actions and aspirations:

- seeking economic security for their families;
- repairing their houses and building new ones;
- growing vegetables;
- planning to keep families small;
- minimizing expenditures;
- taking care of their health;
- educating their children and keeping them and their environment clean;
- building and using pit-latrines;
- drinking tube-well water;
- not taking dowry for their sons' weddings;
- avoiding injustice;
- collectively working for bigger investments for better income;
- helping each other;
- keeping the discipline of these practices;
- practising physical exercise. (Holcombe, 1995)

Group members must demonstrate their familiarity with the Sixteen Decisions before being accepted as borrowers. Gatherings of up to six groups of five meet once a week very early in the morning with the banking representative. They meet at the centre shelter in the village and it is at these weekly meetings that weekly repayment, deposits into savings accounts, and consideration of new loan requests are all conducted (Holcombe, 1995). At the conclusion of the meeting the centre-chief will lead members in physical exercises and in reciting some of the Sixteen Decisions.

Once a new group is accepted as borrowers, the Bank will loan to two of the group on the understanding that all five share responsibility for the loan and the success of the activities it is to fund. If the first two repay regularly then two more will be able to take loans in two months' time. The fifth person is chair of the group. The groups and village centres are central to the operation of the Bank, providing a social structure of support which ensures both that loans are repaid and that where a member gets into difficulty with a project, and hence with repayments, then other members in the group or other groups in the centre will help to find a solution.

In the beginning the Bank lent to men and women, but women were very reluctant to become involved in loan and saving activities:

> When we started, we set out to make half our borrowers women – but when we entered the villages to talk to them, they would run away. They said go away, talk to my husband, I know nothing about money. Some of them had never even touched money. And if the women weren't worried by the possible opposition from the men, they often had to deal with the rumours, such as that we were really Christian missionaries, or part of a sinister government plot to cull poor people. So we had to do a lot of work to overcome these fears, including setting a policy of 'protect the loan and protect the marriage'. After a while, it became obvious that the women actually handled money better than men, and were having more success in its management. We therefore decided that instead of trying to make half our borrowers women, we would make women our priority. (Yunus, 1995)

Now 94 per cent of the Bank's borrowers are women. The Bank loaned its members $400 million in 1997 and it achieved a 98 per cent payback rate. The benefits of the loans and savings reached around 10 million people as each household contains five or six people and they all benefit from the improvements in income and social practices which the Bank enables. Typically, by the end of a few loan periods all the members of the household will find employment in the enterprise that the loan has enabled. Initially, a loan might enable the purchase of a cow for milk which can then be sold, or made into ghee or yogurt. Later, accumulated savings from income will enable a household to purchase a weaving loom, tools and material for furniture-making or for improving production from a vegetable patch, and the household will then begin to establish a self-sufficient enterprise involving manufacture or growing, and selling. The Bank will often provide technical assistance to secure its borrowing in the new enterprise. Vaccination for cows has become widely available to Grameen members and they may also get assistance in marketing their produce or craft goods.

The Bank also loans money for house construction and purchase over a ten-year period at the low rate of interest of 8 per cent which is cross-subsidized by other activities. The land title must be in the name of the woman. Most houses for which loans are given are constructed after a design drawn up by a group of Bangladeshi architects. It is designed to be low cost, to use indigenous materials, to be aesthetically pleasing and to include many clever features such as natural ventilation, efficient use of space, and ability to stand high wind velocity. The Bank also makes a very low-cost form of health insurance available to its members. Poor housing and health in a country much afflicted by floods and cyclones are the commonest reasons why even among the Bank's members some families still do not escape poverty.

In addition to microcredit, Grameen has taken on some larger projects, such as a failing government fish farm, textile design and marketing, and more recently a telecommunications network. Grameen has also developed a form of group farming which allows individual farmers with very small plots to work together as Grameen members, pooling their lands and labour and using credit to improve their produce and output levels, and enabling them to erect storage facilities so they can sell in the market when the price is right. The Bank is involved in these larger enterprises because its members recognize that simply increasing the amount of cash in the rural economy is not enough for fundamental economic change. These larger enterprises provide the members with ways of integrating with the larger economy and of working towards structural economic changes which may ultimately benefit all the poor of Bangladesh (Holcombe, 1995).

The vision and values of the Grameen Bank guide and inform everything that the Bank does. The basic belief is the optimistic one that 'poverty can be removed from the earth' and that the way to achieve this is to target and empower individuals who are poor to 'do their things' and so to get out of poverty (Holcombe, 1995). The fundamental principle is that people like Sophia do not need political re-education or new technologies or even new employment opportunities to be liberated from poverty. They simply need to be empowered to make the changes in their circumstances which they already have the skills to make. Yunus says that he takes a 'worm's eye view' of poverty: 'If I can help one single person it is better than thinking about the whole nation' (Holcombe, 1995). The core technique for organizing around this belief is a model of operation which ensures participation so that the Bank's clients are also its members and owners. Participation in the groups and Bank centres leads to new social and leadership skills which in turn produce empowerment and act as a generator of further social change.

The Grameen approach to poverty alleviation is much simpler than many other development interventions. It does not rely on large inputs of aid, with the usual externally imposed conditionalities. Though the Bank benefits from gifts from overseas donors, it does not rely on them as it does not have a net loss on operations, having a better loan repayment rate than commercial banks. Neither does the Bank rely on external technical expertise or technologies. The key resource is the efforts and skills of the poor themselves once released from the cycle of debt and dependency. Grameen can also claim to be more effective than other forms of development aid. For example, in relation to family planning, Grameen has seen significant reductions in family size among its members for a level (and cost) of intervention which is far lower than typical donor-funded family planning exercises, and without the overtones of control which these exercises carry. According to an in-depth study of the organization, the Grameen Bank works because it values the capacities of its members and its employees. By pursuing this core value the Bank succeeds in putting people in charge of their own lives and their own communities and this is the key to its success in poverty alleviation.

Recovering Local Control and Participation in a Globalized Economic Order

Bangladesh is one of the poorest countries in the world. Its lands and ecology are threatened by years of deforestation in the river valleys of the Himalayas and their foothills north of Bangladesh, which mean that devastating floods have become a regular and tragic feature of life for many of its people. The 1998 floods were, however, unprecedented in scale, submerging more than 40 per cent of the land area of Bangladesh and devastating agricultural and manufacturing activities. This feature of Bangladesh's ecology mirrors the way in which the forces of the global economy have been cascading down on the poor of South Asia, Africa and Latin America with ever-increasing force in the last two decades. But the cascade would not be as fierce in its effects on the poor if it were not for the collusion of a small class of rich people in every country in the world whose interests are more aligned with the international monetary system than they are with the welfare of the people of their country.

The Indian economist Arun Makhijani, like many observers, sees a direct connection between the internal mechanisms which keep the poor in poverty today and the pattern of colonial labour exploitation:

Among the strongest forces perpetuating Third World misery are the divisions that exist between races, genders, religions and classes within Third World countries. Many kinds of severe conflicts, some directly economic (relating to land, employment and wage issues) and some around social and political issues (ethnic, religious and regional divisions), have become widespread. These conflicts are often fanned by segments of local elites or political parties, in a manner quite similar to the divide-and-rule policies which were practised by imperialist rulers of the Third World. (Makhijani, 1992)

The Grameen Bank shows that there is a way to subvert the increasing exploitation and inequality which globalizing finance combined with local moneylenders and low-wage employers and landowners have visited on the poor.

As we have seen, the global financial system is moving closer to a situation where speculative and investment capital, and traded commodities, move around the world with fewer barriers. However, the other key ingredients of economic activity – human labour and land – are less mobile. But a global market can work efficiently only where all factors are mobile. Where they are not, capital will tend to create turmoil, constantly opening and closing factories in the quest for cheaper labour, land and other natural resources. Banks and corporations in the North favour a situation in which high wages in northern economies are subsidized by low wages and cheap raw materials in the economies of the South. However, this requires that producers and consumers in North and South are kept apart by border controls and other mechanisms to restrict the international movement of labour.

International monetary exchanges and regulations, including those surrounding international debt and structural adjustment, operate in such a way as to sustain these hidden and coercive relationships between northern affluence and southern poverty. The internationalization of money in the last twenty years has not been a simple matter of liberalization all round. The US has used its military, financial, political and corporate muscle to bolster the dollar as the effective gold standard in international exchange despite its own giant public debt and trade deficits with the rest of the world. As the value of the dollar, the yen, sterling and the German mark have risen constantly against currencies in the South so the labour, land and raw materials of these countries constantly get cheaper for northern economies to exploit. Thus while monetary accumulation is currently increasing in northern countries, as reflected in the rising value of northern corporations, banks and stock markets, the welfare of the poorest people and their environments in the South is correlatively decreasing. The problem is that global mechanisms of monetary exchange, and money values, do not reflect the true value of people's labour, or of the environments and natural resources that they mobilize.

If we examine the origins of Western business firms we see that, like the Grameen Bank, they were locally based and monitored closely by their local shareholders who at annual meetings could vote out directors or whole boards if they did not approve of their decisions. However, as firms expanded and amalgamated they became less responsive to individual shareholder or local community concerns and more exclusively focused on the maximization of profit.

Today the majority of shares in Western corporations are held by institutional investors and banks. Most banking corporations also originated as local community-based savings and loans organizations which were owned by their members. But once again many of these mutual and member-controlled organizations have become international and non-mutual, like the British building societies which have converted from mutual to non-mutual status, offering big bribes to individual investors who consequently voted for the change in large numbers. Through the processes of takeover and cartelization a spreading network of corporate control and cross-investment between transnational banks, investment houses and corporations has emerged which means that modern global corporations and financial institutions are increasingly removed from democratic or popular control both in the North and the South. And yet these organizations control a growing proportion of global monetary exchanges and global trade.

One way – other than through ownership – in which

communities traditionally exercised control over financial entities was through political regulation, taxes and legal controls. But such is the size and power of many of the global corporations that they can negotiate down taxation, environmental and labour regulations with countries they are proposing to invest in. Many global banks and corporations also make increasing use of 'offshore' tax havens which mean that they can protect their profits from taxation by the countries where these profits originated, and which bear the costs of their generation in pollution and natural resource depletion.

But instead of outlawing tax havens, Western governments have instead responded to global corporate tax evasion and resistance to environmental and labour regulation by lowering the levels of corporation tax, reducing the capacity of trade unions to challenge labour conditions or low wages, and resisting pressure for improved environmental regulation of industry and reduced consumption of energy, timber and other natural resources. Multinational lobbying tends to be focused on the big centres of power in the northern economies, especially Washington DC, and Brussels at the headquarters of the European Union, and it has been particularly successful in making the case for a deregulatory global regime.

As we have seen, the last round of negotiations under the General Agreement on Tariffs and Trade produced a free trade straitjacket under which countries which exploit child or prison labour, or rapaciously degrade their environments, to produce agricultural or manufactured goods can trade on equal terms with countries with decent labour laws and environmental protection. The multinational corporations have also been lobbying for new international rules to police international investment which would grant them a range of legal privileges including immunity from local environmental regulations and labour laws, and limit their liabilities to local and national taxes. Earlier attempts to produce such a set of rules under the proposed Multilateral Agreement on Investment in the Organization for Economic Cooperation and Development (an organization only open to rich nations) have now foundered but Western governments have moved these efforts to the secretive and undemocratic World Trade Organization.

As democratic and political control of corporations and banks has reduced in the last two decades, non-governmental organizations in North and South are exploring new ways for concerned consumers, investors and savers to use their money-power to enhance conditions for poor farmers and producers, and protect environments, in the South. Grameen is a particularly important exemplar of a new approach to money and finance. Similar microcredit initiatives are emerging in many countries in both North and South. One which is common in many northern economies is the credit union where people save and borrow through locally owned and controlled mutual funds which, like Grameen, do not require collateral for credit but rely instead on relationships in the local community as a guarantee of repayment. Through this means the poor are helped to escape from the cycle of debt and high interest in communities in the North as well as the South. Joining and investing in a local credit union is a particularly powerful way for Christians in both North and South to subvert the growing and pernicious power of the global money markets and to reconnect the power of money with the welfare of local communities.

Another important form of this approach is what is known as 'ethical consumerism'. In the UK, Traidcraft has been trading for more than twenty-five years as an ethical trading company. Together with Café Direct, Green and Black, Clipper Tea and other ethical trading organizations, Traidcraft has made it possible for consumers in the UK to purchase coffee, tea, cocoa and craft goods from producer cooperatives in the South at prices which ensure fair wages and proper environmental regulation in the making of the goods.

Traidcraft and Café Direct have also had some success in reaching supermarkets who account for more than three-quarters of UK food retailing and many of whose stores now stock at least three high value fairly traded products – Café Direct, Clipper Tea and Maya Gold Chocolate. There is also a growing number of food cooperatives in Northern Europe and

North America which offer a whole range of fairly traded goods and organic produce, allowing consumers to spend the majority of their weekly food money on goods which enhance environmental and labour conditions in North and South.

The Grameen Bank is also involved in promoting fair international trade on behalf of its members. Its biggest export is of the colourful hand-woven fabric which is called Grameen Check. The cotton yarn is dyed before weaving, making the fabric look and stay beautiful as it is colour fast. Grameen Check is made by 200,000 shareholder handloom weavers, and exported to the USA, Europe and Japan.

The consumption of fairly traded goods represents around 0.5 per cent of the retail sector in North America and Northern Europe. But it represents an important symbolic pointer to an alternative approach to trade and monetary exchange, rather than the one advanced by global financial liberalization and trade deregulation, and one which is growing fast as consumers in the North become more aware of the social and environmental costs of conventionally traded products and foodstuffs. The benefits of fairly traded exchange are estimated to reach around 5 million households in the South involved in coffee, tea and cocoa production, and craft or textile fabrication.

Another form of ethical consumerism, and one which has the potential to affect the lives of even more people in the South than those reached by fairly traded goods, is the concerted lobbying of supermarkets and other retailers by individuals, churches and consumer groups, allied with non-governmental organizations such as Christian Aid, Oxfam and CAFOD, to press for decent labour and environmental standards in the production of their internationally sourced goods. A typical British supermarket sells foodstuffs from over seventy countries worldwide, such as mangetout from Zimbabwe, cut flowers from Kenya, mangoes from Costa Rica and papaya from Ghana. A sports outlet may sell shoes made in Indonesia and China, footballs stitched in Pakistan, shirts tailored in Bangladesh, shorts sewn in Morocco and sports equipment and bicycles constructed in Taiwan.

These goods are often produced by people who receive

wages which do not allow them even to feed their children, and who must endure hazardous conditions in the workplace or on the farm. Through concerted lobbying and campaigning, aided by media exposure of appalling conditions in many developing-country factories and farms, non-governmental organizations and ethical consumer groups in the USA and Europe have shamed companies like Nike and Reebok into investigating and improving labour and environmental standards in factories where they source their products. As a result of campaigning in the UK the three largest supermarket groups – Tesco, Sainsbury and Safeway – have agreed to create codes of conduct with their suppliers which will involve higher labour and environmental standards in relation to the food and other products they source in developing countries.

Voluntary agreements of this kind resulting from consumer lobbying are valuable achievements. But the holy grail of trade regulation is the World Trade Organization itself. As we have seen, this undemocratic organization is in urgent need of reform so that its internationally binding policing of world trade will allow countries to resist trade in goods which have been produced in ways which damage environments or neglect human rights and proper labour standards. Civil society groups in both North and South are lobbying their governments to pressure for change in WTO rules of operation so that proper labour and environmental standards, as defined by the International Labour Organization, and Agenda 21 at the Rio Earth Summit, will not be treated as obstacles to free trade but rather laid down as preconditions under which international trade will in future be conducted.

Similar efforts are being made in some quarters to introduce ethical concerns into international banking and investment. A small but growing proportion of funds and savings in the North is being deposited in ethical investment schemes. The terms of ethical funds vary but typically they claim to avoid investing in arms or tobacco, or in notably polluting industries such as chemical, oil, energy and automobile production.

Efforts to introduce ethical criteria into the operation of international financial institutions such as the World Bank and the International Monetary Fund have met with very little success. The former World Bank economist Herman Daly describes how he tried, and failed, to persuade the Bank to recognize that there are environmental limits to economic growth and that sustainable development is not compatible with the blind pursuit of economic growth (Daly, 1996). Similarly, as we have seen, the Bank's commitment to poverty eradication has always taken second place to its espousal of economic growth and deregulation as the primary aims of its coercive influence over developing nations.

The key reform to the developmental strategy of the Bank and other institutions which economists like Daly commend is the abandonment of the current measurement of economic growth in terms of Gross Domestic Product and the adoption of a new way of assessing economic performance which measures sustainable development (Daly, 1996). 'Sustainable development' is a phrase which has acquired a large range of meanings and in particular it is often used by economists and politicians to speak of sustainable *economic growth* rather than *sustainable* development. When environmentalists first coined this phrase they were refering to a kind of development under which consumption and production in the present do not undermine the life chances of other living persons or degrade their environments, nor undermine the life chances and environmental quality of future generations.

The problem with present measures of economic growth and activity, Gross Domestic Product being the most common, is that they do not include the costs of production or consumption activities as these are visited on environments, individuals or communities adversely affected. A sustainable measure of economic activity would factor in irreplaceable natural resources which an activity consumed and human costs arising from pollution, unemployment or poor health and safety. Until monetary measures of activity are redesigned in this way, the measurement of economic growth in the money economy will continue to be a poor guide to the growth of human life quality or the preservation of the diminishing natural resource base of the planet.

Another key reform to the global economy is the reimposition of regulations and taxes on the free-floating pool of speculative money whose daily transactions, as we have seen, can exceed 1 trillion dollars. George Soros, the billionnaire currency speculator, has proposed that international regulation of speculative capital flows is an urgent requirement if these flows are not to continue to wreak havoc on national economies, and even bring about a global financial collapse (Soros, 1997). And some countries are beginning to do this unilaterally, and often in the teeth of opposition from the 'Washington Consensus'. Chile has imposed reserve requirements on all capital inflows into the country, except foreign direct investment. This creates an important disincentive to speculative capital flows, particularly in relation to foreign exchange speculators. Malaysia has reimposed capital controls as a consequence of the destabilizing impacts of currency speculation on the Malaysian *ringgit* and the Malaysian economy.

The economist James Tobin proposed the imposition of what has come to be known as a Tobin tax on all speculation on foreign currency. The Tobin tax would impose a global surcharge of 0.25 per cent on all speculative purchases of foreign currencies. This would discourage very short-term purchases of currencies for speculative gains and would encourage money to stay in one place long enough to do some good. Preparedness to impose the Tobin tax could be used as a condition of a country using the services of the International Monetary Fund and the World Bank.

Such ethical approaches to regulating the impact of global finance and trade on the welfare of local communities and environments are, however, only part of the answer to the alleviation of world poverty. They attempt to address structural imbalances in the global economy which reflect power imbalances rooted in the long and exploitative history of colonialism and the related development of global capitalism. But such reforms will only be effective against the countervailing forces of inhuman and environmentally damaging globalization if they are teamed with a larger project to reintroduce democratic and moral controls into regional and local forms of monetary exchange system and their impacts on natural resources and human communities.

If communities of the poorest in sub-Saharan Africa, South Asia and Latin America are to benefit from such structural changes, grass-roots approaches to democratizing the local and regional economy, such as the Grameen Bank, are all the more important. The very poor in sub-Saharan Africa and South Asia are rarely beneficiaries of inward investment or international trade and, as we have seen, increased trade in cash crops resulting from structural adjustment has done little to improve their circumstances.

Grameen represents an alternative approach to development which begins with the existing resources and creativity of the poorest, rather than relying on aid-funded external interventions, or international trade and investment. It is also a form of development that is focused on the local community and the village. Earlier in this century Mahatma Gandhi championed the *swadeshi* or local economy in the context of the struggle of the Indian people against the British Raj; 'the true India,' Gandhi said, 'is to be found not in its few cities but in its seven hundred thousand villages. If the villages perish, India will perish too' (Kumar, 1996).

The Indian economist Satish Kumar identifies the principles of self-reliance and village-based democracy as the essential features of *swadeshi*:

> Gandhi's vision of a free India was not of a nation-state but a confederation of self-governing, self-reliant, self-employed people living in village communities, deriving their livelihood from the products of their homesteads. Maximum economic and political power – including the power to decide what could be imported into or exported from the village – would remain in the hands of the village assemblies. (Kumar, 1996)

Gandhi saw the village as a mini-republic which through its community self-sufficiency would meet most of its own needs and be able to resist the tyranny of market forces. Gandhi's vision of economics was the complete opposite of the British colonial vision of a centralized industrial system. He was also opposed to mechanical manufacture and farming. Work with hands was dignified work whereas the service of machines was soul-destroying. Machines and large corporations are instances of the quest for profit which is driven by individual greed:

> In contrast, a locally based economy enhances community spirit, community relationships and community well-being. Such an economy encourages mutual aid. Members of the village take care of themselves, their families, their neighbours, their animals, lands, forestry, and all the natural resources for the benefit of present and future generations. (Kumar, 1996)

Just as the global economy promotes greed, inequality and conflict over resources, Gandhi saw the local economy as promoting peace and social harmony, and the development of the human spirit. Sadly, modern India is increasingly embracing free trade and militarism, as witness its recent experiments with nuclear bombs. But the principles of *swadeshi* live on in many villages in South Asia and are being reborn in the barefoot banking of the Grameen Bank.

Mainstream economists often contend that calls for a return to local economics and self-reliant village communities represent a utopian throwback to a supposed golden age which was never so golden, and which is in any case not realizable in an increasingly global system. However, the resurgence of local economics is not limited to South Asia. Grameen-type microcredit schemes have sprung up in many countries in the South in the last decade. And similar efforts to revive the local economy are beginning to emerge in Northern Europe and North America where many communities are also suffering from a form of structural adjustment as global capital abandons high wages and effective environmental regulation for cheaper and unregulated locations in the developing world. The resultant unemployment and underemployment have fostered the creation of Local Exchange Trading Schemes (LETS) where people swap their skills, for example as decorators, vegetable growers, drivers or tutors, by using local currency units which are exchangeable for other services. These units are sometimes also tradable in local shops and businesses but cannot be exchanged for money and have no value beyond the local economy. LETS schemes give people who have been left out of the globalizing money economy a new means for sharing their skills, and hence new purchasing power. Like the Grameen Bank they represent the relocalization of money, and the creation of an exchange system which encourages community self-reliance and brings individuals isolated by lost work or earning power back into relationships of mutual benefit.

Another form of local economics is known as 'community supported agriculture' or 'linking farmers with consumers'. The principle here is that food produced on farms close to urban communities is sold directly to consumers, thus cutting out the transportation and retailing costs, and the enormous waste associated with large supermarket trading practices (Imhoff, 1996). Community supported agriculture draws local communities back into relationship with farmers and the land, and also helps to shift farming in a more sustainable direction as most community supported agriculture schemes involve organic or low-intensity produce.

The growth of community supported agriculture reflects growing concern at the pesticides and chemicals left in food as a consequence of the commercial and government-led intensification of farming in the last thirty years in both North and South. Community supported agriculture also reflects a desire in urban and rural communities to remake the connections in the local economy which have been broken by nationwide and international trading practices. In some schemes, consumers even offer their labour on farms as payment for foods instead of cash. In this way, community supported agriculture also encourages a more hands-on approach to farming, keeping more people in touch with the land and reducing dependence on expensive and energy-consuming machines. Community supported agriculture represents a move towards remaking the local economy which is also beneficial to low-wage or unemployed people and to the environment.

The democratization of the mechanisms of trading and exchange from the local to the global is the key to reorienting the global money and trading system so that it promotes the welfare of the poorest, and of local communities and the environment. This democratization will only be fully realized when local communities recover control over their own livelihood and natural resource base. But this recovery of community self-reliance, of connections between local land regions and livelihood, and of exchange activity based in face-to-face relationships is not just an economic programme for poverty alleviation. It is, also, as Gandhi suggested, a spiritual project, whose links with the religious practices and beliefs of Christians, as well as Hindus and Muslims, are clear to theologians in Asia and around the world.

Restoring Personhood to the Poor

Democracy or 'good governance' is often held out as the answer to poverty in sub-Saharan Africa, Latin America and South Asia, but India, Pakistan and Bangladesh all have forms of multi-party democratic government which have been in existence for many years. However, the model of development which these countries have embraced has not succeeded in eradicating poverty because it has been focused on industrialization, urbanization and individual consumption rather than on the economy of the village and the basic needs of the poor. While the urban-based middle classes have expanded, systematic poverty in the villages and the vast slums of South Asia has not been properly addressed.

The Indian theologian K. C. Abraham argues that the problem lies with the exclusion of the poor from real political influence and the corruption of vested interests:

> The masses are nowhere near the centres of power in our political process. As we have noted earlier, a powerful elite has come to dominate the political scene. Their only concern is to further their vested interests. Not only do they keep the masses away from the decision making process, but they also fail to solve the basic problems of mass

poverty, glaring inequalities, growing unemployment and rising prices. When there arises any organized effort by the masses to redress their grievances it is brutally suppressed. Assuming more and more executive power and enacting laws that curtail basic freedom, the elite-controlled governments have become authoritarian. Thus the state which is meant to be an instrument of justice and freedom, has itself become the major source of violence and terror. (Abraham, 1983)

If we look into the origins of modern democratic practice in the West we find it has deep roots in Christian theology and in particular in the Reformation idea of the sovereign individual who is indwelt by the Spirit of God rather than dependent on priests or other human institutions for the experience of grace (Northcott, 1998). According to the post-Reformation advocates of democracy it is people collectively who, under God, confer sovereignty on the state. And so where the state usurps its authority the people have a right to withdraw their consent to its laws and diktats.

But it is impossible for people mired in poverty and exploitation to exercise this popular sovereignty. As the South African theologian John de Gruchy explains, 'democracy cannot be sustained and flourish where there is large-scale poverty. Poverty, not the poor, is an enemy of democracy' (de Gruchy, 1995). Consequently, the imposition of democratic structures on cultures and regions characterized by mass poverty may only serve to enhance division and give the rich new structures and ideologies with which to justify the lot of the poor, as Abraham so incisively observes.

As we have seen, the globalization project of financial deregulation and the international 'free' market is sometimes presented as a utopian response to global poverty and to the failure of statist and often authoritarian government to redress poverty. Free-market economists argue that states fail in poverty eradication because they are working against the laws of nature which are manifest in market forces. These forces are said to ensure the survival of the fittest in the competitive struggle for resources and wealth. Instead of societies organizing collectively to raise up the poor, it is argued that collective action and regulation must be kept to a minimum to allow more space for individuals to create wealth and foster economic growth which will ultimately lift the poor out of poverty.

Underlying this ideology of the market is a false theology of humanness. According to market ideology, the lone individual is empowered most when freed from mutual and community responsibilities and relationships. And the ultimate source of empowerment is the interaction between individual effort and the invisible hand of impersonal market forces liberated by deregulated finance and trade. This ideology represents the forces that redeem the human condition from poverty and failure as distant, external and impersonal. In proposing that social and political communities must cede authority to these impersonal forces if they are truly to advance their own welfare, market ideology grants ultimacy to the 'non-god' of money-power.

There is much in common between the impersonal non-gods of the market and free trade, and the impersonal non-god of fatalism which is so deep in the cultures of South Asia as described by the Indian theologian K. C. Abraham:

> The Indian masses are under the spell of a culture that views man as a creature subject to the laws of nature and as one who is caught in a wheel of destiny from which there is no escape. Poverty, ill treatment and exploitation are all accepted with passive resignation as part of one's destiny or fate. (Abraham, 1983)

M. M. Thomas argues that the central contribution of Christianity to Asian culture is the discovery of personhood and of the community of persons which corrects the impersonal fatalism which views life as an endless circle of karma, a struggle between impersonal forces over which individuals and communities have no control. The concept of the person is linked by Thomas with the emphasis on historical purposiveness in Christian thought which gives hope in human endeavours for progress in redemption from suffering and poverty. Thomas identifies the impact of these values on Asian religions and in secular liberalism, Marxism and nationalism as equivalent to a spiritual awakening: 'This spiritual awakening, this awareness of the personal and the historical, which has come to us in India through the impact of the West, is in a sense related to Christ who is informing the Western culture' (Thomas, 1976).

An earlier Indian theologian, P. C. Mozoomdar, similarly argued that the incarnation of God as a person in Christ has particular power in relation to the Hindu belief that person-hood dissolves in death when it is absorbed into divinity:

> Christ did not destroy his personality. Christ did not come to teach us to destroy our personality. Christ did not teach the miserable doctrine of absorption and annihilation; on the contrary, Christ has perpetuated and glorified his own personality and that of his followers by establishing between God and man the eternal relation of filial progress. Man's personality is then truly human and complete when it is not opposed to God, and being one with the Father is our genuine freedom. (Mozoomdar, 1883)

Christian belief in a personal God has particular relevance in the Asian context because it gives vital meaning to the personhood of the poor which both Asian religious fatalism, and the new fatalism of the global market, tend to dismiss. The poor are not merely the objects of external forces beyond their control. They are persons who share the divinity of personhood as revealed in the incarnation of Christ. And as the Sri Lankan theologian Tissa Balasuriya argues, the essence of Jesus' concern for the poor and for justice was his own belief in their personal worth:

> Jesus stressed the personal worth of all human beings regardless of their social condition or status. He helped persons understand that their worth did not depend on the prevailing social values of power, wealth, social position, physical strength, intellectual acumen, legal eminence, or even religion. Merely external laws had no moral binding

force before God if they were unjust. This is the foundation
of universal human responsibility and freedom.
Historically it has been the ultimate stand of champions of
freedom and justice over the centuries. Jesus laid down the
principle of the rights of every human person as a child of
God and a bearer of free will. (Balasuriya, 1984)

It is significant that the values which inform the Grameen Bank
approach to poverty eradication are so similar to the Christian
values identified by Asian theologians as crucial to social
transformation in the Asian context: recognition of the personal
worth and creative potential of poor people, optimism and
hopefulness that the condition of poverty is not inevitable and
can be transformed, and participation in the struggles of the
poor toward social transformation. The prevailing and often
caste-informed prejudice toward the poor in South Asia is
radically challenged by the Bank which requires its employees
to live in the villages of the poor:

> One officer told of opening a Bank Branch in Rangpur
> Zone. When he first arrived he and the other Bank
> employee, a Bank Assistant, were able to find only a thatch
> roof hut to share. On the first night a huge rainstorm came,
> pouring through the roof, soaking their bedding and
> possessions. Later they obtained a proper building with a
> tin roof but lacking electricity. It served as office and
> residence. (Holcombe, 1995)

As Susan Holcombe comments in her in-depth study of the
Bank:

> Grameen staff share a knowledge of the reality of the lives
> of the poor, a knowledge that sets them apart from other
> educated people, including members of their own families
> who do not understand why Grameen requires honesty,
> long hours and postings away from the home District.
> (Holcombe, 1995)

The emphasis on participation also reflects Grameen's valua-
tion of human community and solidarity as means to over-
coming the impersonal forces that keep the poor in poverty. By

building up group relationships as a precondition for borrowing, and by building up a strong community philosophy among the members and employees of the Bank, Grameen fosters a sense of belonging among its members and a sense of mutual commitment to poverty eradication. As one area manager said, the 'greatest happiness is finding improvement for poor people' (Holcombe, 1995).

It must be acknowledged, however, that while the Grameen Bank seems to have encapsulated these Christian values in its organization, the traditional mission churches in South Asia have often failed to do this. Christian missionaries expended considerable effort on education and medical care among high-caste Indians in the hope that their conversion would draw the lower castes along also. But in practice few high-caste Indians were attracted to Christianity, while low-caste, untouchable or Dalit peoples were attracted in significant numbers (Devasahayam, 1992). And they were attracted by the very egalitarian values which repelled high-caste people. As Devasahayam comments, the attraction of Dalits to Christianity amounted to a series of mass movements which bewildered the missionaries and transformed the nature of the Indian Christian church 'from a tiny, urban, educated community of mixed social origins to a predominantly poor, rural, illiterate Dalit community':

> The Good News appealed to Dalits because it proclaimed Christ's love even to the outcastes and the socially rejected. They were happy to associate themselves with an almighty Father who was more powerful than the demons of whom they were afraid and were appeasing. They were also attracted by the values of equality, fraternity and self dignity enshrined in the proclamation of the Gospel. They certainly hoped for betterment in social, economic, intellectual and religious realms. (Devasahayam, 1992)

Despite the numerical dominance of Dalits in the churches in South Asia, caste prejudice and discrimination still persist among Christians. Dalits often worship in separate churches or are given separated seating in places where there is one church.

They are not invited to communion until all non-Dalits have received and they are discriminated against in matters of church government and leadership. And separate cemeteries for Dalits and non-Dalit Christians are common in South India.

Dalits have always preferred egalitarian religions to caste-based ones and hence many Dalits embraced Buddhism and later Islam earlier in Indian history. Many of the peoples of Bangladesh are descended from Dalits who were converts to these non-Hindu religions. However, the presence of Dalits in the churches of South Asia is only now issuing in a new Dalit consciousness and a Dalit theology which emphasizes the personhood of the Dalits, rejects the fatalism which views poverty and discrimination as their caste fate and encourages them to take responsibility for their own transformation (Prabhakar, 1994). Dalit theology also has a significant stress on the corporate aspect of the church and the collective responsibility of all members of the church for social justice and transformation:

> The Dalit situation would emphasise the essential *community* nature of the church, the *koinonia*, a *community of the faithful and a community of life* wherein each member and all members together, priests and people alike, live the Gospel and fulfil in word and deed the mission of the Church, which is to 'witness to the love and liberating power of God in Jesus Christ in the contemporary society'. (Prabhakar, 1994)

This Dalit understanding of the nature of the Church places a particular emphasis on the power of people in groups to transform their social relations from division into unity and from prejudice or even hate into love. Through history, Christian churches have often failed to live up to this calling but this must not prevent us from acknowledging the power of Christians working in communities to sustain hope in social transformation and collective action to bring it about.

In many non-Western contexts in Asia, Latin America and Africa the church is being reborn from below in what Leonardo Boff has called 'ecclesiogenesis'. The new churches from below, whether they are Pentecostal house churches in the *favelas* of Latin American cities or Dalit churches in outcaste communities in South Asia, are demonstrating a new sense of empowerment, often expressed in terms of a distinctive understanding of the working of the Spirit of God who is experienced as powerfully present in the lives of each individual member of these new churches and in collective praise and worship, and who is also said to unite the members together into communities of transformative love and social solidarity. This distinctive dynamic of individual empowerment and collective mutuality and solidarity is central to the enormous and growing appeal of the Pentecostal form of Christianity which has become the fastest growing Christian style on the planet (Cox, 1996).

This joint emphasis in the Dalit and Pentecostal expressions of church on individual empowerment and community solidarity is also important in a proper view of governance and moral responsibility in relation to global economic forces and the management of natural resources. Too often the alternatives are posited as either impersonal market forces and deregulation, or national and international governmental structures and regulatory procedures. But in both cases, when taken to extremes, there is a tendency for control of natural resources, livelihood and governance to be removed from local communities and deferred on to large impersonal forces or systems whether financial or bureaucratic in nature. The net effect is that local communities are disempowered, and particularly individuals and communities of the poor who do not have power to lobby or to influence the vested interests which both corporate and bureaucratic actors so often sustain.

The theory and especially the practice of 'church from below' point to an alternative approach which is focused around the empowerment of individuals in local communities, whether in villages or in cities. It relocates action for social transformation, poverty eradication and natural resource conservation in the face-to-face relationships and collective actions of local communities empowered to take their destiny in their own hands. Above all it suggests that the keys to poverty eradication lie in the creativity and relational resources of ordinary people, and of poor people, and that waiting for structural change 'from above' will not bring the justice and the material uplift they seek.

This is not to say that the need for international development aid is over. But what the poor of Latin America, Africa and South Asia actually want is not more aid, which is often diverted in any case into debt rescheduling, but freedom from dependence on the debt conditionalities and unfair trading practices imposed by the resource-greedy North, freedom to rebuild their own lives, lands and communities. As Gandhi observed, it was precisely as a consequence of colonial dependence that the villages of India became as impoverished as they were:

> Before the British advent India spun and wove in her millions of cottages, just the supplement she needed for adding to her meagre agricultural resources. This cottage industry, so vital for India's existence, has been ruined by incredibly heartless and inhuman processes as described by English witnesses. Little do town dwellers know how the semi-starved masses of India are slowly sinking to lifelessness. Little do they know that their miserable comfort represents the brokerage they get for the work they do for the foreign exploiter, that the profits and the brokerage are sucked from the masses. (Gandhi, 1922)

The Grameen Bank and other microcredit and fair-trade initiatives which empower the poor in South Asia once again to weave and sew and find a dignified livelihood in their villages are in a sense simply trying to undo the legacy of more than three hundred years of colonialism in South Asia. It would be tragic if the outcome of present-day globalization, and in particular the enforcement of so-called free trade which is not free but rigged towards the North, were to repeat the 'crime against humanity which is perhaps unequalled in human history' which was the destruction of the indigenous industry and livelihood of the villages of South Asia by the British Raj (Gandhi, 1922).

Sources

K. C. Abraham (1983), 'The Role of Ideology in India' in *Towards the Sovereignty of the People: A Search for an Alternative Form of Democratic Politics in Asia – A Christian Discussion* (Commission on Theological Concerns, Christian Conference of Asia: Singapore)

Tissa Balasuriya (1984), *Planetary Theology* (London: SCM Press)

Harvey Cox (1994), *Fire from Heaven: The Rise of Pentecostal Spirituality and the Reshaping of Religion in the Twenty-First Century* (London: Cassell)

Herman Daly (1996), *Beyond Growth: The Economics of Sustainable Development* (Boston: Beacon Press)

V. Devasahayam (1992), 'The Kingdom of God in India' in V. Devasahayam (ed.), *Dalits and Women: Quest for Humanity* (Madras: Guruklal Lutheran Theological College and Research Institute)

Mahatma Gandhi (1922), 'Statement in the Great Trial of 1922' in *The Selected Works of Mahatma Gandhi: Volume Six, The Voice of Truth* (Ahmedabad: Navajivan Publishing House)

John de Gruchy (1995), *Christianity and Democracy: A Theology for a Just World Order* (Cambridge: Cambridge University Press)

Susan Holcombe (1995), *Managing to Empower: The Grameen Bank's Experience of Poverty Eradication* (London: Zed Books)

Daniel Imhoff (1996), 'Community Supported Agriculture: Farming with a Face on It' in Jerry Mander and Edward Goldsmith (eds.), *The Case Against the Global Economy and For a Turn Toward the Local* (San Francisco: Sierra Club Books)

Satish Kumar (1996), 'Gandhi's Swadeshi: The Economics of Permanence' in Jerry Mander and Edward Goldsmith (eds.), *The Case Against the Global Economy and For a Turn Toward the Local* (San Francisco: Sierra Club Books)

Arjun Makhijani (1992), *From Global Capitalism to Economic Justice* (London: Apex Press)

P. C. Mozoomdar (1883), *The Oriental Christ* (Boston, MA)

Michael S. Northcott (1998), 'Christian Futures and the State of Britain' in Ursula King (ed.), *Faith and Praxis in a Postmodern Age* (London: Cassell)

M. E. Prabhakar (1994), 'The Search for a Dalit Theology' in James Massey (ed.), *Indigenous People: Dalits – Dalit Issues in Today's Theological Debate* (Delhi: ISPCK)

George Soros (1997), 'The Capitalist Threat', *Atlantic Monthly* (February).

M. M. Thomas (1976), 'The Struggle for Human Dignity as a

Preparation for the Gospel' in Douglas J. Elwood (ed.), *What Asian Christians Are Thinking: A Theological Source Book* (Quezon City: New Day Publishers)

Muhammad Yunus (1995), Public Lecture, Sydney University.

Organizations

The Fairtrade Foundation Suite 204, 16 Baldwin's Gardens, London, EC1N 7RJ
Tel 0171 405 5942
Fax 0171 405 5943
E-mail: fairtrade@gn.apc.org

Traidcraft Kingsway, Gateshead, Tyne and Wear, NE11 0NE
http://www.traidcraft.co.uk/news12.htm

Oxfam Trading PO Box 72, Bicester, Oxon, OX6 7LT
http://www.oxfam.org.uk/fair_trade.htm

Christian Ethical Investment Group 90 Booker Avenue, Bradwell Common, Milton Keynes, MK13 8EF
Tel: 01908 677 466
Website: http://www.gaeia.u-net.com/ceig01.htm

Grameen Bank
http://www.grameen.com/bank/

7 Towards Ethical Development

Development through Redistribution in the 'Land of Coconuts'

My name is Joseph Verghese and I live in my family home in a small village in Kerala, which is the state on the southwestern tip of India. Ours is one of the most heavily populated states in India. Like most people in Kerala we own the small patch of land on which our house is set. It is a simple structure with two rooms which we built with the help of our neighbours. The walls incorporate a clever pattern of holes between the bricks which let the breeze through and cool the inside. The roof which is made from dried coconut branches and leaves also forms a canopy front and back which keeps the tropical sun off the walls and gives shaded space and shelter from the monsoon rain where we cook, eat, and sit out with our neighbours. The house is in a compound which is not large but it has just enough space for three coconut trees, a mango and a papaya tree. The mango produces yellow fragrant fruit for most of the year. We rely on it, especially towards the end of the dry season when the rice is running out and other food is very expensive. Sometimes we might have mango for breakfast and dinner – raw in the morning, fried in the evening. We also try to keep a banana plant growing but the shade of the other trees is often too much for it.

We don't own much by Western standards but we never go hungry. Besides the house we have pots and pans, a bench and some stools, two beds, the stove, some agricultural tools, baskets, and plastic bowls for doing the washing and washing ourselves. We use oil lamps when we want to read after dark. We also have a bicycle. One house in the village has a television and a video and we all crowd round when they get a new Indian movie. Though our life is simple, and economically poor, our place would probably look quite inviting to those Westerners who fantasize about a simpler ecological lifestyle. Like much of Kerala, the village is really a collection of houses under a canopy of coconut trees which provide a constant supply of food and drink.

The smells in the early evening are delicious. We cook fish, when we can get it, in coconut milk and flavour it with coriander, cloves, green chilli and cumin, mostly using spices and herbs we can pick near the village. You can hear the wind whispering in the leaves of the coconut. There is also the sound of running water as there is a canal running through the village.

Kerala is mostly a very low-lying region and there are lots of canals and rivers, many of them navigable with flat-bottomed boats we use to ferry goods and people around. We also catch fish in the canal. There is a small Hindu shrine and in the next larger village there is a small church where my family goes on Sundays as we are Marthoma Christians. There is also a mosque in the next village. Kerala is a very multi-religious state, but with much more religious harmony than in other parts of India. When the BJP (Hindu nationalist party) came to try to get votes for their anti-Muslim Hindu fundamentalism they did not find any supporters in this village, and they did not get one candidate elected from Kerala.

I am just nineteen and have finished school. My brother went off to college but I did not do so well in school and have been looking around for a job. My mother cooks food for a roadside stall. She makes sweet sticky rice. She turns it into small snacks by wrapping portions into pieces of banana leaf. She takes these on the bus to Cochin where she sells them to office workers at lunchtime. My father rents around an acre of paddy field and we plant rice there twice a year thanks to the new seed varieties.

There is a lot of unemployment but I just got work on a new government horticultural scheme. The idea is that we use the paddy fields to grow vegetables between rice crops when otherwise the land would be sitting idle. This scheme is good because it provides work for the youths and at the same time reasonably priced vegetables for sale in the local market. We grow brinjal (aubergine or egg plant), ochra, tomatoes, peppers, chillies, onions and various kinds of greens. We don't make much money between us but life in the village is good. We have the security of owning our own house compound and my father has a long-term tenancy on the paddy.

We all benefited from a really good education. At the senior school I attended more than a third of the children went on to college or even university and everyone attends both junior and senior schools in this state – it is not just the rich or the middle classes but even the poorest who do this. This is largely thanks to the communist governments who have been elected on and off for more than thirty years. The government also invests a lot in local clinics so all children are immunized against the killer diseases like polio, and women can get access to free birth control. Families are typically just two children, like ours. This is also because parents can be sure that their children will survive them and look after them in their old age because the health and nutrition programmes of the clinics mean that very few die in childhood, unlike in the rest of India.

We learn a lot in school about hygiene and public health and the importance of keeping family size small. We also learn a lot about the different states of India, and other parts of the world where, even though there is sometimes more wealth than we have in Kerala, the poor people suffer from diseases and malnutrition which we do not see here any more. I hear from my relatives that even in rich cities like New York and Boston there are beggars and homeless people on the streets. You will not see this in Kerala and we are very proud of living in a fair society where no one is driven to beg.

In school we also learn to question and to challenge our politicians if things are not going right. It was because the communists challenged age-old traditions like caste and landlordism that things got better for my parents' generation. And now they have learnt to challenge when things are wrong as well. For example, in our village the road was not made up and in the dry season it was very dusty. Whenever a motorcycle went past, or even a push-bike, the dust would be thrown up and end up in our houses. In the wet season the road used to turn into a muddy stream and became unusable. The villagers got together and passed round a petition about the road which they sent to the government. They also held peaceful demonstrations at government offices and so finally the road was made up.

There are now some changes in Kerala that are not so good. This is because India has begun to welcome the big Western companies, like multinational pharmaceuticals and soft drinks companies which used to be kept out by laws which were meant to protect Indian businesses, farmers and fisherfolk. This change is affecting us here as well. So for example the government food shops, which used to sell low-priced food to poor people, are being run down and this is really hitting us hard as we relied on the shop in the dry season when our rice ran out and other foods were too expensive for us. This is why the government started the scheme to grow vegetables for low cost that I am working on. Also the price of coconuts and of natural rubber has fallen and this has affected our income as we cannot make much from selling them.

The economy used to be organized around the village in Kerala. We still have a wonderful thriving village community and the best times are when everyone contributes to a communal celebration like Deepvali or Thaipusam and the celebration lasts for a few days and old friends and relatives come back to the village to join in. When I am with my friends and family in these gatherings we can forget about our other worries. We appreciate that we have some riches here that other people, who have more money than us, do not have. But we are also worried at the trends we are now seeing. We don't want our village, and other villages in Kerala, to be messed up by these global economic winds which we can't control.

Fairness and Sustainability in the Local Economy

As we have seen throughout this book, the model of economic development that Western economists, development banks and official aid agencies have consistently encouraged or coerced developing countries into following, with a drip-feed of aid projects and bank loans and loan conditionalities, is based on the trickle-down theory of economic growth. Official aid and development loans have been used mostly to build infrastructure like roads, dams and power plants and to fund large agricultural and industrial projects with the idea that economic growth will be stimulated, jobs created and the poor ultimately will benefit. The assumption is that the only way to improve the lot of the poor is by building infrastructure with which to attract industrialists and encourage new businesses who will then help the poor by giving them jobs, and paying taxes which governments may then use to help the poor.

However, the focusing of development monies and state budgetary management on policies such as deregulation and privatization which are designed to promote economic growth rather than redistribute wealth has not reduced but increased global poverty in the last twenty years. This approach has also involved the systematic destruction of natural resources, and especially of forests and fisheries. During the 1998 monsoons large areas of China, Bangladesh, India and Vietnam, and later Central America, were affected by exceptional flooding and millions of people lost their homes and livelihoods. Climatologists and ecologists have noted a big increase in such 'natural' disasters in the 1990s. They are partly connected with the growth-driven over-exploitation of natural resources, which wiped out whole forests that formerly acted as natural protection from flooding. They are also connected to larger changes in the world's weather systems associated with the phenomenon of global warming caused by too much production of carbon dioxide and other greenhouse gases produced in industrial societies (Northcott, 1996).

Because of global liberalization of trade and capital markets, investment capital now tends to go where taxes and labour and environmental regulations are lower. As a consequence the traditional model of development through economic growth is no longer redistributing wealth from rich to poor as it had done until financial deregulation in the mid-1970s. And this is why Kerala is such an important story, a story not just of a non-governmental organization or a development bank with an alternative approach to development, but of a semi-autonomous political entity in one of the poorest, and most populous, nations on earth. The recent history of Kerala indicates that, contrary to the ideology of economic liberalism, democratic states, even very poor ones, can use the mechanisms of taxation, public sector investment, market regulation, education and social programmes to reduce poverty (Franke, 1994).

Since electing their first communist government in 1957, the people of Kerala have pursued an alternative model of development. Instead of economic growth as the primary aim, they have opted for redistribution of the existing wealth of this very populous state. They have been so successful in this alternative approach that the current life expectancy of a Keralan male, at 70 years, is only two years below the average life expectancy, 72 years, of a male in the United States of America, the richest country on earth.

The anthropologist Richard Franke has drawn up a physical quality-of-life index with which to compare life quality between countries. Franke found that Kerala's score was 88 (out of a possible 100), higher than the average score of persons living in the monetarily much richer United States of America (Franke, 1996). The US score is brought down by growing extremes of poverty and wealth which generate social unease and stress for both rich and poor. Kerala's score is as high as nations with much higher mean per capita incomes such as Singapore and Taiwan (McKibben, 1995).

The average income of Keralans is difficult to estimate precisely because of the contribution to some households made by Keralan children working abroad, but government figures estimate it at around $320 per person per annum. This means Keralans have an average income roughly one-fiftieth of people in Britain or one-seventieth of people in the USA. The average income of Keralans makes them one of the middle-ranking Indian states in terms of money wealth. But begging, destitution, malnutrition and homelessness, which are common throughout even the least poor states of India, are virtually unknown in Kerala. Unemployment is a major problem, as are rising food prices, but Keralans have found ways of redistributing what limited wealth they have fairly and equitably such that even the poorest do not starve or lack shelter.

Wealth redistribution began with land reform, initiated by the first communist governments of Kerala in the late 1960s. More than 1.3 million tenant farmers benefited from the land reform law. Landowners were compensated and many of them put the money into the further education of their children who supported them in their old age when rents no longer did (McKibben, 1995).

Some argue that the roots of present-day Kerala's success in beating poverty lie in its earlier colonial history. In the nineteenth century, the Keralan Rajahs gave Keralan tenant farmers an unusual amount of control over the land in order to stimulate agricultural production and increase revenues for themselves and the British. This approach had the effect of encouraging tenant farmers to drain swamps and marshes and build the foundations of what is now a very efficient, if still low-income, agricultural subsistence economy. However, without the land reform of the post-colonial economy, under communist rule, there is little doubt that Keralans would not enjoy the quality of life that they do today.

Another central feature of the development model of Kerala is education. Every child in Kerala goes to school. The environmentalist Bill McKibben noted on his visit to the state that in the morning 'every road in Kerala is lined with boys and girls walking to school'. And he comments, 'of all the subtle corrosives that broke down the old order and gave rise to the new Kerala, surely none is as important as the spread of education' (McKibben, 1995). The government also sponsored a series of statewide adult literacy programmes which were staffed by more than twenty thousand volunteer tutors who reached out to every village in the state. Today Kerala is one of the few places in contemporary Asia with a 'total literacy' rate, which the United Nations defines as a population where 95 per cent can read and write (McKibben, 1995).

There is a political intent in the extent to which education and literacy have been set at the heart of Kerala's development. The left-leaning politicians who have governed Kerala for the past thirty years, communist and non-communist alike, believe that when people are educated, and educated in the right way, they will themselves question and begin to overthrow the old order of hierarchy, landlordism and casteism, and reject the servility and exclusion which characterize the lot of the poorest throughout India. Literacy classes were designed to teach people about politics and society. Through drama and dance as well as reading and writing lessons, people learnt how to hold democratic representatives and government officials to account and how to get officialdom to meet their needs, as in the case of the metalled road in the story above. As a result Keralans are very articulate and political people. They see politics as something which involves everyone, in contrast to much of the rest of India, and many societies in the West, where politics is so often limited to the ballot box and the cult of the political leader.

As well as giving the illiterate and the powerless a sense of their political rights, literacy classes were designed to teach people about their responsibilities, and not least their responsibilities for public health, personal hygiene and family size. The government also invested in a network of local clinics, giving every woman access to free family planning and health care, and enabling a very successful statewide immunization programme for children (Jeffrey, 1992). Infant mortality has consequently fallen to levels equivalent to those in North America. This has enabled parents to limit their families typically to two children, thus helping to reduce population pressure in an already very crowded region. Kerala has a statewide population density approaching that of some Western cities with nearly two thousand people per square mile.

Another key plank in government efforts to reduce poverty by redistributing existing wealth was the provision of 'fair-price' shops where people may purchase rations of rice below market price, their rations being set in proportion to how much or how little paddy land they own themselves. These efforts to distribute food fairly have meant that despite the real poverty of many Keralans, and their very low average incomes, diseases of malnutrition such as kwashiorkor are almost unknown in Kerala (McKibben, 1995). Kerala has achieved this because it has avoided the kind of agricultural reforms foisted on so many countries in the South by Western bankers, where prime agricultural land has been taken out of subsistence farming and given over to the commercial growing of cash crops for export.

Kerala is not the only state in the South which has achieved this kind of development miracle while purposely turning its back on the traditional economics-led approach to development. Eritrea, the state which won its independence from Ethiopia after a long and bitter civil war (and is still threatening Ethiopia in border skirmishes), has pursued a not dissimilar strategy. Eritrea, like Ethiopia, is one of the world's poorest countries, even poorer than Kerala. And yet its capital city Asmara is a model of cleanliness and order. It has working public services, almost no beggars and very little crime, unlike most other capital cities in Africa (Hirst, 1998).

The long years of war instilled in Eritreans the values of self-reliance and survival through sharing. These values have shaped their approach to post-war development. For example, the formerly very splendid Italian railway system was completely broken up during the war. Bits of track were strewn over the countryside and the engines rusted up. Foreign offers to fix it would have required loans in excess of $100 million. Not wanting to become dependent on foreign loans, Eritreans rejected foreign 'aid' and set about repairing the system for themselves. Young people on national service scour the countryside for old rails and sleepers, and even the old and rusted Italian steam locomotives are being repaired using local skills and parts run up on old metal lathes. The government uses a period of forced national service for all young people as a source of labour not only for military training, but also for repairing the railways, planting millions of trees, repairing eroded hillside terraces and building microdams to help conserve water for local crop irrigation.

The Eritrean government took the same self-reliant approach to food distribution. From a system developed in the war of food hand-outs, which were reliant on and controlled by foreign aid donors, the government fashioned a new agricultural and food distribution programme which initially involved a compulsory (and rather harsh) food-for-work programme, and later a work-for-money programme. Both programmes have been wound up as Eritreans are now more or less feeding themselves. Once again the key to this programme was the rejection of control by foreign aid organizations and a swift move back to self-reliance in food (Tesfagiorgis, 1995).

Another key to Eritrea's success, in addition to self-reliance, is its approach to politics. Like Kerala, Eritrea has a lively and popular political culture born partly from its long struggle for independence. The new constitution has yet to be drawn up and is discussed avidly by people up and down the land. The present political leaders are mostly former guerrillas, pay themselves reasonable salaries and avoid corruption. The president receives the highest salary at £490 a month, which is a tiny fraction of the salaries of other African presidents. Eritrea's politicians live simply without the trappings of chauffeur-driven cars and air-conditioned offices. Uniquely in Africa, corruption is virtually unknown in Eritrea. Only two cases of fraud were reported in 1997 among government officials. The tax system also works effectively and progressively as a means to wealth redistribution, with a 49 per cent personal income tax for the higher paid (Hirst, 1998). And people pay their taxes, which is not common in other, more corrupt, and less effectively governed nations in the South.

'Good governance' is a popular phrase among development experts and bankers, particularly in the era of structural adjustment. But foreign bankers have little conception of the debilitating effect on the cultural identity, integrity and political morale of peoples subjected to the degrading levels of economic control exercised by northern creditors over heavily indebted nations. Constant reliance on outside aid and loans, and now on the forced economic programmes of foreign bankers, is deeply subversive of good governance and this is an important reason why good governance is rarely to be found in structurally adjusted countries in the South.

Colonialism itself encouraged servile and corrupt political leadership and put down more independent-minded and effective politicians. Post-colonialism in the form of development aid, bank loans and multinational investment has often tended to encourage precisely the same kind of politics to thrive. It is partly because they have eschewed international aid and loans, and the Western model of economics-led development that Eritreans, like Keralans, have a largely corruption-free and transparent approach to governance.

Another important feature of development Keralan- and Eritrean-style is sustainability. Land is rightly seen as the key development resource. Immense efforts are put into conserving land, and in Eritrea's case, into repairing its lost fertility. The economic aspirations of the people are closely linked to the products of the land, and not to a Western-inspired dream of industrial development. The traditional style of economics-led development assumes that the affluent consumerism of the North can eventually be spread to all the peoples of the earth. But in reality this is a myth. There are not sufficient natural resources to provide the current wasteful form of Western consumer society for all, even if it were desirable.

To give just one example, the land area needed to produce timber and animal fodder sufficient to sustain present levels of consumption of timber, paper and meat in Britain is more than seven times the size of the British Isles. Much of the land area which is used to sustain current consumption levels of primary commodities is located in the South, as it has been since the days of Empire. Even if there was sufficient land area for such high natural resource use to be shared by all the earth's current 5.8 billion people, we now know that the earth's life systems do not have sufficient capacity to absorb all the waste and pollution which affluent consumer societies are generating. Global warming may not be a major threat to affluent societies located in the temperate zones of the North but environmental disasters are already impacting very severely and tragically on the lives of millions in the tropical regions of the South which are much more sensitive to climate change.

The stories of Kerala and Eritrea demonstrate that it is possible to improve the life quality of the poorest without waiting for the trickle-down effect of industrial-led development. Too often these improvements never appear. And because of the debt crisis, trickle-down has turned into a trickle-up effect where resources are stolen from the poor and given to the rich.

These stories of Kerala and Eritrea also demonstrate a kind of development which does not require the uprooting of forests, the destruction of fisheries, and the enforced migration of peoples from self-reliant agrarian villages to the misery of urban-industrial slums as land is forcibly acquired for commercial and industrial farming. As Bill McKibben notes, Kerala is a model of the original meaning of sustainable development: living on the earth in such a way as not to consume natural resources which other people need for their own welfare either now or in the future (McKibben, 1995). In both Kerala and Eritrea the ideal of social justice is given practical expression through the fair distribution of natural resource wealth, which in turn promotes sustainable natural resource use.

This connection between social justice and ecological sustainability is a central feature of models of alternative development which many non-governmental organizations, and some development experts, are increasingly advancing as a counter to the growth-led development model promoted by the World Bank and other development banks and official aid organizations. The growth-led model is destructive of both human communities and natural resources because it proceeds on the pure logic of capitalism which, left to its own unregulated devices, is a system of value and surplus accumulation. This system involves the continual consumption of natural resources to the point where scarcity advances the need for technological change. It also involves the continual uprooting of settled human communities who must constantly move and adapt to the industrial cycle of business start-ups and closures, technological change, monetary inflation and recession.

The model of alternative or 'another development', a phrase

first coined by the Dag Hammarskjold Foundation, involves the attempt to put human needs and welfare, and the conservation of natural resources, above the requirements of the economic system of surplus accumulation (Carmen, 1996). Proponents of another development argue that conventional development is intrinsically destructive of human communities and of natural resources because its measures of success are fundamentally flawed. When we measure human development through the purely quantitative measures of neoclassical economics we will often be measuring things which are actually indicative of failed development or what is sometimes called 'maldevelopment'. Destroyed forests which produce flooding and local climate heating, plundered fisheries which remove people's local and sustainable livelihoods, eroded soil from monocrop plantations, all produce pluses in the balance sheets of companies and the GDP of nations, but their net outcome is a reduction in human development, not an advance.

Underlying the traditional development bias towards economic measures of human welfare is the ideology which says that human happiness is produced and collective welfare is advanced by having and consuming more. By contrast, advocates of another development argue that the true sources of human happiness are to be found primarily in non-economic goods such as human relationships, the experience of community, and the autonomous expression of creativity in the pursuit of biophysical security, livelihood and social order (Northcott, 1996). Conventional development results in 'maldevelopment' because it destroys natural resources, living space and cultural integrity through which traditional 'undeveloped' communities pursued these non-economic goods.

Critics of maldevelopment argue that this destruction of autonomous and self-reliant communities, and of the natural resources which they formerly shared and managed, is not an incidental but an intentional outcome of the development process. According to the economic historian Karl Polanyi, capitalism has always proceeded in this way, first uprooting and destroying local autonomous communities and their traditional rights to natural resources, and then turning those resources into commercial profit. From the beginning of the industrial revolution state and legislative power were used by the capital and landowning classes as means to increase their access to and control over both natural resources and human labour (Polanyi, 1945). Advocates of another development argue that this painful transition from peasant to industrial society cannot be replicated throughout the world because there are not enough natural resources for every society to undergo this transformation. They also argue that, while democratic recognition of human and property rights may have been insufficiently developed in the eighteenth and nineteenth centuries to have prevented the dehumanizing excesses of capitalism in early industrial Europe, we cannot allow the same immoral denials of human rights to be visited by Western banks and corporations on our global neighbours as we approach the twenty-first century.

Maldevelopment is above all immoral development. Its world-wide supremacy has, as the social ecologist Murray Bookchin argues, 'turned us into moral cretins' (Bookchin, 1986). Resisting this global immorality will require citizens of democratic countries in the North to urge their governments to commit to an ethical approach to development and international trade, even though this requires some reduction in the pursuit of growth in the economies of the North.

A number of writers have begun to flesh out the principal characteristics of a model of ethical development which sets the well-being of persons and the environment above the economics of growth and quantity (Verhelst, 1989; Latouche, 1993; Carmen, 1996; Trainer, 1996; Daly, 1996). Much of the substance of the following ten rules of ethical development (in their critical and constructive aspects) has been discussed elsewhere in this book.

The Ten Rules of Ethical Development

1. Conventional development measures its success in quantitative economic terms which ignore human well-being. Ethical development uses non-economic measures of human life quality – for example, life expectancy, educa-

tional attainment, variety of diet, quality of relationships, cultural expression – as the measure of its success.

2. Conventional development places a higher value on having than on being, and on consumption than creativity. Ethical development values human creativity and being in community above the consumption of mass-produced artefacts.

3. Conventional development values the mass organization of livelihood through wage labour in the formal economy over informal 'uneconomic' activities such as the nurture of children, the sharing of hospitality and participation in religious festivals. Ethical development values the autonomous, informal and non-economic activities of households and local communities in the pursuit of livelihood and social exchange above exchanges of labour and cash in the formal economy.

4. Conventional development mobilizes state power in order to create 'free' markets – in labour, natural resources and artefacts – which operate independently from the relational networks and moral sensibilities that characterize traditional household and kinship networks and exchange relationships. Ethical development affirms the embedding of economic and material exchanges (for example, the sharing of food or cultural artefacts) in morally charged networks of relationships between households and between local villages and communities.

5. Conventional development affirms the economistic assumption that human needs for material wealth and comfort are infinite and insatiable. Ethical development regards fundamental human needs – for shelter, affection, security, creativity, communication and transcendence – as involving great variety in their expression but requiring finite physical resources to satisfy them. The insatiable character of modern consumerism is the outcome of the destruction of non-economic sources of satisfaction and fulfilment in industrialized societies.

6. Conventional development values free trade in foods, commodities and artefacts above national autonomy and self-sufficiency. Ethical development promotes national,

regional and local self-sufficiency in foodstuffs and other essential goods. It promotes international trade in artefacts and commodities which have been produced by workers who are fairly remunerated and work in healthy conditions, and without detriment to the environment.

7. Conventional development sees no relationship between the quantity of human economic activity, and of money in circulation, and the physical resources and limitations of the biosphere. Ethical development sees the human economy as a subsystem of the earth's ecology. It regards the quantity of money, goods and services in circulation, and the waste products they produce, as limited by the carrying capacity of the earth.

8. Conventional development promotes the consumption of natural resources to the point of destruction, or to the point where the capacity of natural systems to absorb waste and pollution is exhausted. Ethical development promotes the conservation of increasingly scarce and fragile natural resources such as topsoil, tropical forest, ocean and river fish stocks, by affirming local community access to, and control over, natural resources, and particularly of land and fisheries.

9. Conventional development treats people as means to the end of economic growth. Millions of people suffer eviction from their homes or ancestral lands, mass hunger, slum-living and forced or bonded labour in the collective quest for economic growth. Ethical development follows the golden rule of morality which is that people must not be treated as means but as ends in themselves.

10. Conventional development promotes the material well-being of the one billion richest people on earth over the security and freedom of three billion poor people. Ethical development seeks to use and conserve natural resources so as to promote the well-being of all living persons without detriment to the capacity of future persons also to realize similar levels of well-being.

The Folly of the Governance of Money and the Theology of Responsible Government

The fundamental characteristic of the dogma of the global free market in finance and goods is that it promises the political utopia of human freedom and universal welfare by non-political means (Gray, 1998). In the name of this dogma, indebted nation states in the South, and all forms of political governance which are sustained within them, are being coerced by their creditor bankers to reduce their collective efforts to express responsible government and pursue the common good. The aim of their northern creditors is to allow money, markets and private economic entities – corporations – to have more control over their people and their natural resources. Given this increased control, the bankers urge, money and corporations will, by promoting economic growth, ultimately deliver improved welfare for all.

A similar process of adjustment of human communities to markets and the requirements of corporations, and of the 'rolling back' of government power is also, putatively, under way in the North. But as John Gray and others have pointed out, the ideology of deregulated markets in the North has in practice involved the conferral of greater powers on central government over the governed, not fewer (Gray, 1998). The reason is simple. The social disruption, unemployment and injustice that the untrammelled market imposes on human societies, and on their natural environments, causes such social upheaval and unrest that more, not less, coercion is required to be exercised by states over their citizens in order to protect the institutional mechanisms of the free market, and especially corporations and their propertied owners, from its victims.

It is no coincidence that police forces have acquired more coercive technologies, and grown significantly in size, in those countries which have most actively pursued the market society – the USA, the UK, Australia and New Zealand. Nor is it a coincidence that the numbers of poor people in prison in these countries have multiplied, or that the numbers of private security personnel have burgeoned. As we have seen, a similar process is under way in the South. As governments have foisted pauperization on their people, in the name of structural adjustment to prices and corporate needs in the global 'free-trade' economy, so they have also invested more heavily in military and policing hardware – hardware which is willingly supplied by their creditors in the North in exchange for new lines of credit.

At the conclusion of this book we need to remind ourselves of the central truth that talk of free markets and deregulation tends to obscure. This is that money, markets, economies and trade, whether local or global, are not natural processes, nor are they governed by invisible and incontrovertible laws. Rather they are social constructs which are the outcome of an intricate network of political, bureaucratic, legal and social arrangements. Money or markets can never be truthfully described as *de*regulated. Without public regulation they would not be able to function, nor would they have any authority over those who use them or participate in them as owners and traders, consumers and debtors. All of these entities exist by no other power than the political intent and capacity of local communities and nation states to sustain them: by protecting property and sustaining legal contract, by legitimating the supply of money (whether publicly or privately generated), by guaranteeing trade between distant partners, and by enforcing debt.

It is ironic then that official international institutions, themselves publicly funded and ordered, such as the World Bank and the International Monetary Fund, acting on behalf of governments in the North, should have sustained for more than twenty years the free-market ideology that less government is better government, and that markets and corporations are more effective agents of collective welfare than democratically elected politicians, or bureaucrats such as themselves.

In recent World Bank reports and documents, alongside the dogmas of deregulated money markets, liberalized free trade, privatization of public services and the economic advantages of less government, it is now possible to read of the growing interests of the Bank in 'good governance', and in what they call 'sustainable development'. However, the economic programme pursued by the Bank and the Fund continues to involve the substitution of economic management for political government, at the cost of mass pauperization and environmental destruction.

The contrast between the relative order and fairness of the self-reliant and semi-independent states of Kerala and Eritrea and the difficulties of those client states of the Bank and the International Monetary Fund such as Somalia, Bolivia, Brazil, Zaire and Peru which have most closely embraced structural adjustment prescriptions could not be greater. Despite the real poverty of the former, measured in terms of per capita incomes, we see political governance being responsibly expressed in a collective movement towards wealth redistribution, communal self-reliance and sustainability, the key elements of ethical development. In the latter we see economic management in the form of financial deregulation and liberalization of markets in labour and natural resources being imposed by Western bankers as a substitute for political governance. As a consequence we see improving life indices in those states which have retained their independence from the Bank and the International Monetary Fund, and worsening indices of welfare in the lives of the majority of their citizens and in the condition of their natural environments in those whose sovereignty has been undermined by debt and structural adjustment.

The recent demise in liberal ideology in the West of the legitimacy of the state as the responsible manager of the wealth of nation(s) is one of the most notable features of political and economic theory in the late twentieth century. The earliest understandings of the legitimacy of the authority of government and the state in the Christian West, as in the Jewish and Muslim Middle East, and in the Confucian, Buddhist and Hindu Far East, were theological in origin. It may be that the decline in support in the West for the role of the state as the responsible moral agent of certain collectively agreed goods, such as wealth distribution and nature conservation, is not unrelated to declining religious participation in Western countries. It will be helpful then at the conclusion of this book to explore anew the theological and ethical roots of the concepts of political authority and good governance.

The Christian tradition covers a range of stances with respect to the authority of the nation state from outright rejection of tyrannical states or empires to total complicity with the rule of certain states and empires whose sovereignty and community were sometimes judged as coterminous with the political being of the Church, and even with the Kingdom of Christ.

One important strand of Christian political reflection involves the belief that Christians owe no fundamental allegiance to the nation state because Christ has conquered and put down all earthly principalities and powers. Christians are those who recognize that Christ alone is King, and their essential political responsibility before his return to judge the earth is to proclaim his Lordship to the world. On this view Christians may live in certain political entities, they may vote or pay their taxes, but they should not expect that the kinds of moral values – such as love, equality and justice – which are to characterize relationships between Christians, will commonly find expression in the politics and economics of modern secular nation states. This approach to politics was common among the Christians who were martyred at the hands of the tyrannical government of the Roman Empire in the first three centuries of the Christian era. Among the persecuted churches of that era, the Empire was most often seen and experienced as the Antichrist, the opponent of the saints and the destroyer of the mission of the Church.

This negative theology of the state has been influential at various times since the early centuries, and particularly so among the more radical groups which emerged at the Protestant Reformation, such as the Anabaptists and later the Mennonites. For these groups it was the Holy Roman Empire (the Church of Rome) which was the Antichrist. Contemporary exponents of this kind of approach to politics (though not to the Church of Rome) would include the Mennonite theologian, the late John Howard Yoder, and to a certain extent the influential North American Methodist theologian Stanley Hauerwas (Yoder, 1972, Hauerwas, 1991).

An alternative and much more influential strand of Christian political theology involves the belief that, although Christ has indeed 'put down the mighty from their thrones' and led into captivity the principalities and powers of this world, none-theless the authority of kings or governments remains as a surrogate for divine rule and judgement until the second coming of Jesus Christ which will bring this present age to a close. On this view Christians do well to pray for the capacity of rulers to maintain their authority so that they will be able to uphold social order, in the context of which Christians will be enabled to pursue the mission of Christ and witness to his Lordship, and to the values of God's kingdom, in their own local and ecclesial communities and in civil society.

This view of the authority of earthly rulers is reflected in the writings of the Apostle Paul in Romans 13 (and in the first letter to Timothy commonly attributed to Paul) wherein Paul calls on Christians to pray for rulers and to regard them as the agents of divine judgement and wrath against evildoers. Paul as a Roman citizen seems to have rejoiced, for the most part, in the freedom which the Roman Empire gave him to travel widely in preaching the gospel throughout the Empire and founding churches. Many of the Church's early theologians took the view that the coincidence of the incarnation of Jesus Christ with the zenith of the Roman Empire was indicative of divine providence. The existence of this global Empire enabled the message of Jesus Christ to spread throughout much of the world from Middle and Northern Europe through North Africa and even, on some accounts, to the Far East in the first three centuries after the death of Christ.

In the varied experience of Christians at the hands of Rome, which moved from martyrdom in the first three centuries to religious freedom in the fourth and fifth centuries, these political theologies – from Empire as Antichrist to Empire as providential guarantor of the Church's missionary freedom – were to compete for theological prominence. Some theologians combined the two, seeing the persecution of the Church as part of the providential ordering of the world, a divinely ordained instrument to keep the Church holy and pure, through the blood of the martyrs, until Christ's return to judge the world. After the conversion of the Roman Emperor Constantine to Christianity, it is the providential account of Empire which is pre-eminent. The Church and the Empire come to be viewed as mutual partners in furthering the mission of Christ, each with their respective vocations (O'Donovan, 1996). The Church witnesses to the mission of Jesus Christ in the world, and the Empire may enable that mission by maintaining social order and by being modest in its own exercise of secular authority.

This partnership between Church and state in the mission of Christ was to issue in that political form which came to be known as Christendom. Christendom is widely identified with the tyrannies and crimes against humanity of European imperialists, and therefore its theologians and formulations are mostly dismissed as a possible source of post-colonial political theology. However, in a rereading of the theological and political achievements of Christendom, Oliver O'Donovan argues that the modern practices of constitutional government, of government by popular will, and above all of responsible moral governance, all originated in the Christendom era. These practices, he contends, provide important resources for the recovery of a modern political theology which can affirm the possibility and legitimacy of ethical government in a world in which economic management is increasingly substituted for responsible political governance (O'Donovan, 1996).

As we have seen throughout this book, the tendencies of the late modern world are towards forms of global investment, trade and treaty which gradually reduce the powers of states responsibly to order the lives of their citizens and the natural resources of their lands, to the common good of the people and of non-human species. Globalization of this kind represents a serious threat to responsible government, and not just in its most pernicious form – globalized debt and globalized economic control of debtor by creditor nations. The globalization promoted by the multinational character, and supranational size, of deregulated financial services and global corporations represents a serious challenge to the capacity of all nation states responsibly to promote and sustain the welfare of their citizens and their environments.

A theological response to globalization must include then a theological justification of government. It need not be tied to its current modern expressions, such as the nation state or private domains of governance such as multinational corporations and banks. But it can clarify the characteristics and appropriate role of responsible, as against tyrannical, government and authority whether expressed by local, regional, national or supranational bodies or powers.

The first word that the gospel utters about the powers of governance is of course the most definitive one, and this is that Christ has subjected all principalities and powers to his divine authority. Christ is the only true ruler, the only one whose Kingdom can evince the unstinting loyalty of Christians because his Kingdom is the only one which is characterized by divine justice, which favours the poor and the marginalized. From the annunciation of the incarnation of God in Jesus, come the first gospel words with political substance, the words of the Magnificat:

[the Lord] has shown strength with his arm;
he has scattered the proud in the thoughts of their hearts.
He has brought down the powerful from their thrones,
and lifted up the lowly;
he has filled the hungry with good things,
and sent the rich away empty.
(Luke 2.51–3)

This expression of the kingly rule of Christ has subsequent political implications in terms of later Christians' understanding of the origin of the authority of responsible government, that is government which upholds the good and punishes wrong-doing. Paul takes the view that the power of the 'governing authorities' (Romans 13.1), by which he refers to the Roman Empire, has an authority over Christians analogous to the authority of the Mosaic law because it is instituted by God.

The law was given by God that humans might know sin, and therefore know their need of grace and redemption in Jesus Christ. The law could not save humanity from sin but it was still a crucial part of the divine plan for humanity. Similarly, the authority of the Empire was not viewed as a saving authority. Nor was its exercise seen as reflecting conceptions of Christian love and mercy (Romans 13.8–10). However, it was a rule which had the authority of divine judgement, analogous to the judgement exercised by the Mosaic law. And, like that judgement, if Christians avoided wrongdoing, the apostle Paul argued, they would not come into conflict with legitimate worldly authority. The governing authorities were said though to have only a temporary authority of judgement, for they ruled in the interim between the ascension of Christ and Christ's return at the end of history, which Paul believed was an imminent event (Romans 13.11–14).

This view of the interim nature of political authority did not suffice in the succeeding Christian centuries where the Church found itself at times in conflict, but increasingly in partnership, with governing authority. O'Donovan argues that the key contribution of Christendom to the evolution of political authority in the West is the idea of constitutional government. Under this conception, government authority is derived from law, not from property (which may have been acquired by coercion) or from inheritance (as in the case of the inherited monarchy which predominated in Europe until after the Renaissance). According to O'Donovan, the development of Roman law within Christendom expressed the belief that all law is derived from, and should be shaped by, divine law: 'The legislative activity of princes, then, was not a beginning in itself; it was an answer to the prior lawmaking of God in Christ, under which it is judged' (O'Donovan, 1996).

We now live after Christendom but we still live in a world of law, both national and international, which has been at least partially shaped by Christian principle, precisely because of this connection between human legal codes and divine law. This insight is of considerable value in political theology for it establishes a basis on which Christians can both critique bad government, and also discern, support and even campaign for good government, both locally and globally. And this approach provides clear theological principles for distinguishing between morally responsible government and tyranny. As O'Donovan puts it, bad government involves 'the substitution of partial or sectional interests for the good of the whole', and tyranny is the worst case of bad government where a single leader substitutes his own private gain for those of sectional interest (O'Donovan, 1996). Thomas Aquinas argued that since 'law is the structure of public good' no law can be derived from tyranny, and further that it is legitimate for tyrants to be overthrown (O'Donovan, 1996).

Correlatively, O'Donovan argues, it becomes possible to find in the laws and actions of certain governments, or international institutions, evangelical and Christian principles and intentions, and Christians should not hesitate to do this, any more than they should hesitate from criticizing bad government. Many of the nobler outcomes of secular politics can be traced to Christian ideas and practices, including the recognition of the rights of persons and communities to life, liberty and sustenance, and the legitimacy of social arrangements which restrain inequality and promote the common good.

But modern rights talk is problematic because it ascribes original rights to individual persons, whereas for Christians the rights of persons are derivative on the being of God, and on a social world ordered by divine law. As O'Donovan argues, subjective ascriptions of rights reflect a 'demoralised conception of society' (O'Donovan, 1996). They also sustain a realm of rights claims which is open to manipulation by the wealthy who may assert their rights in ways which oppress the weak. This cornering of rights by the powerful may be observed in recent history as wealthy private corporations have been granted the status of fictive persons in modern legal systems.

This status of fictive persons has conferred rights on corporations which often trounce the rights of local communities whose rights to sustenance, to an unpolluted environment, or to decent working conditions, may be abrogated by such corporations.

Similar rights have been conferred on transnational corporations and banks in the legal regulation of international trade and finance, much of which has been constructed to defend the economic freedom of large multinational corporations, financial service providers (including currency speculators) and banks. Thus the World Trade Organization under its current terms of operation forbids discrimination between goods produced by people in countries where workers' rights have been respected and others where workers' rights have been denied. Even worse, under WTO rules, and the North American Free Trade Agreement, which operates between the nations of North and South America and provided a model for the proposed Multilateral Agreement on Investment, no nation is able to discriminate between traded goods on the basis of either environmental or human rights considerations.

Through this new body of international law, the capacity of nations to advance the common good of their own citizens through constitutional legal arrangements is being systematically subverted. Furthermore, this new body of law is being developed at the behest of corporations and bankers in the richest countries in the North, and in clear contradiction of other international legal codes, such as those of the United Nations Convention on Human Rights, international labour law as promulgated by the International Labour Organization, and the environmental treaties concluded at such international fora as the Earth Summit at Rio de Janeiro and the Climate Convention at Kyoto.

Modern Christians in both North and South live 'after Christendom'. But nonetheless, on the basis of the kind of political theology that O'Donovan espouses, it is possible to find theological grounds for affirming many of the achievements of modern liberal societies and nation states. The legal codification of the natural rights of citizens to shelter, employment, food and a decent environment, and taxation and welfare systems which distribute wealth according to natural right and not just according to the power of private interest, are political and economic achievements which may therefore be said to have theological validity and foundations.

However, in the human stories and economic facts recounted throughout this book we can see the international emergence of an increasingly amoral political economy in which the interests of corporations and financiers are raised above those of the common good of political communities. In other words, we can see a new form of tyranny emerging in international politics which is subverting the capacity of nation states to express good, moral and responsible government.

In this situation, Christians and churches throughout the world are not only bound by the gospel to seek to express an alternative ethic in their own communities. They are also required to engage in the common and shared task of upholding the legitimacy and necessity of good government. As O'Donovan argues, what is at stake in the amoral abandonment of political authority, as the means through which societies can organize themselves for the common good, is the authority of Christ himself. For when Christians proclaim 'the victory of Christ over the ruling powers' they also defend the 'provisional role' of the powers against those who would undermine governing authority in the name of economic management or some other amoral programme:

> For the impact of Christ's victory shaped not only how rulers' tasks were thought about in Christendom, but how society itself, claimed for its own fulfilment by the rule of Christ, was understood. Early-modern liberalism implied not only lawful government but a community susceptible to it; it comprised a set of expectations about how human beings might live together. (O'Donovan, 1996)

And as O'Donovan goes on to say, these expectations were not only formed by the impact of the law of God in law-governed societies but also by 'the other stream of divine law, the law of the Spirit of life in Christ Jesus' which 'shaped civil society too, and so helped change the forms of government from below into those which would accord with the presence of Christ's authority in society' (O'Donovan, 1996).

We have seen at many points in this book how non-governmental organizations, including churches and other groups in civil society, have been most vocal and active in resisting the threats to human welfare represented by the tyranny of money, debt, international finance and global free trade. What we find in O'Donovan's distinctive approach to political theology is a theological affirmation of the significance of this resistance to tyranny. We also find in it an affirmation of the role of civil society groups, through dialogue or partnership with their governments, in upholding the natural right of citizens to liberty and livelihood, and the duties of political communities, local as well as national, to organize their affairs so as to express the common good of their citizens, if necessary against the rights of corporations, bankers or other private interests. And just as this approach to political theology offers concepts and discourses with which to defend morally responsible government against the current ideologies of globalization and liberalization, so it also offers discourses with which to identify evil when it finds expression in political or economic power.

The traditional theological name for an agent of government which requires uncritical obeisance or worship, and which oppresses the mass of the peoples of the known world in the name of its interests and designs, is Antichrist (O'Donovan, 1996). This term may well be used to name the current phase of global capitalism in which the free movement and uncontrolled expansion of global finance is advanced by powerful corporate and governmental actors even when it produces, as it is doing in the late 1990s, such a degree of financial chaos and misery as to undermine social order, and the natural right of citizens to life and livelihood in the majority of countries in the southern hemisphere (and hence the great majority of people on the planet). Christians have a duty to name this evil for what it is, and against it to continue to affirm the authority of the ascended Christ who is Lord of Lords and who has dethroned the principalities and powers of this world.

In naming this evil we have already begun to subvert its power over its victims. Even the manipulators and agents of this power have begun to own its tyrannical and malign tendencies. The international currency speculator George Soros, in *The Crisis of Global Capitalism*, argues that the world financial system has experienced a succession of crises in the present decade as a consequence of the imbalance between the power centres of deregulated global capitalism – New York, London, Frankfurt, Tokyo – and the less-developed countries with which we have been primarily concerned in this book (Soros, 1998). Soros is also critical of the amoral tendencies of markets left to their own devices, of the destructive effects of contractual relationships on democratic and familial relationships and networks. Soros argues that we need a new democratization of global political agencies, and in particular of the United Nations, to rein in the otherwise destructive power of global markets. An important feature of such democratization would be a new juridical body, located within the UN, which would be empowered to hold global corporations to account for human rights and environmental abuses. Currently individuals or communities in developing countries which have been maltreated by global corporations often have no opportunity of seeking legal redress because they have no status in the courts where these mostly northern corporations maintain their headquarters, or insufficient financial resources to mount legal challenges in courts in the North. Soros also argues that we need to preserve areas of our local and national life – such as education and health care – where market values are not allowed to replace relationships of trust, care and compassion.

Christians will, however, continue to urge the case that global financial and trading arrangements, and not just local or national public service provision, should express Christian values of trust, care, justice and compassion. Christians in both North and South will continue to press governments and bankers to remove the political bias expressed in global financial markets towards the shoring up of banks and bad debts at the expense of the peoples of the South whose lands and children are dying because of these debts. Christians will continue to look for mechanisms to trade fairly and ethically with those who have become their neighbours through the mechanisms of global trade. Christians will continue to require companies in whom they invest their savings or pensions to improve the ethical orientation of their production and trading systems.

We may feel that such actions are insignificant in relation to the secular powers which oppose justice for all the peoples of the earth. But when connected and undergirded with worship and prayer to the God of gods such actions express the deep and spiritual connection between the intentions they express and the struggles of the powerless all over the world for justice.

Prayer connects us in a global spiritual community which is deeper than the 'community' of international finance. Prayer for economic justice affirms the spiritual orientation of human life, and the spiritual character of the revolution in human societies which the quest for material justice requires. Worship reminds us not only that the struggle is with principalities and powers, but also that the origin and destiny of human being is hidden with Christ in God. The Christian hope is not a false optimism that things can only get better. But it does involve a recognition that neither financial nor political systems in this world have ultimate power. For God alone is the true source of power in the universe, and the recognition of this spiritual truth dethrones the power of the non-god – money – to distort God's world and to enslave its peoples.

Sources

Murray Bookchin (1986), *The Modern Crisis* (Philadelphia: New Society Publications)

Raff Carmen (1996), *Autonomous Development: Humanizing the Landscape* (London: Zed Books)

Herman E. Daly (1996), *Beyond Growth: The Economics of Sustainable Development* (Boston: Beacon Press)

Richard Franke (1994), *Kerala: Radical Reform as Development in an Indian State* (Oakland, CA: Food First Publications)

Richard Franke (1996), *Life is a Little Better: Redistribution As a Development Strategy in Nadur Village, Kerala* (South Asia Books)

John Gray (1998), *False Dawn: The Delusions of Global Capitalism* (London: Granta)

Stanley Hauerwas (1991), *After Christendom* (Nashville: Abingdon Press)

David Hirst (1998), 'The ancient train of empire that carries Eritrea's new dreams', *The Guardian*, 9 September

Robin Jeffrey (1992), *Politics, Women and Well-being: How Kerala Became a Model* (London: Macmillan)

Serge Latouche (1993), *In the Wake of the Affluent Society: An Exploration of Post-Development* (London: Zed Books)

Bill McKibben, *Hope Human and Wild: True Stories of Living Lightly on the Earth* (New York: Little, Brown and Company, 1995)

Michael Northcott (1996), *The Environment and Christian Ethics* (Cambridge: Cambridge University Press)

Oliver O'Donovan (1996), *The Desire of the Nations: Rediscovering the Roots of Political Theology* (Cambridge: Cambridge University Press)

Karl Polanyi (1945), *Origins of Our Time: The Great Transformation* (London: Victor Gollancz)

George Soros (1998), *The Crisis of Global Capitalism* (New York: Little, Brown)

Gebre Hiwet Tesfagiorgis (1995), *Emergent Eritrea: Challenges of Economic Development* (Addis Ababa: Red Sea Press)

Ted Trainer (1996), *Towards a Sustainable Economy: The Need for Fundamental Change* (Oxford: Jon Carpenter)

Thierry Verhelst (1989), *No Life Without Roots* (Eng. trans., London: Zed Books)

John Howard Yoder (1972), *The Politics of Jesus* (Grand Rapids, Michigan: Eerdmans)

Organizations

The following organizations are campaigning for global economic reform and welcome interest and subscriptions from individuals:

Bretton Woods Project PO Box 100, London, SE1 7RT
Tel: 44-171-523-2117
Fax: 44-171-620-0719
E-mail: bwref@gn.apc.org
Contact: Angela Wood

Center of Concern 1225 Otis St. NE, Washington, DC 20017
Tel: (202) 635-2757
Fax: (202) 832-9494
Contact: Jo Marie Griesgraber

The Social Crediter 16 Forth Street, Edinburgh, EH1 3LH
http://www.gil.com.au/va/scss

Shared Interest 25 Collingwood Street, Newcastle upon Tyne, NE1 1JE
Tel: 0191 233 9101
Operates savings accounts for members willing to lend to micro-enterprise schemes in the South.

Five Talents Fund c/o OCMS, PO Box 70, Oxford, OX2 6HB
Makes grants to micro-enterprise schemes in the South.